Southern Devotions

A Selection of Devotional Writings

Southern Devotions

A Selection of Devotional Writings

Printed and bound in the United States of America. All composition rights reserved.

ISBN 9780971185029
Copyright©2023 by Kenneth M. Lee

Material included herein shall not be used for commercial intent; nor shall it be reproduced for or within information storage and retrieval systems.

Kenneth's devotions have been published in *The Upper Room* (Christmas Eve, 1999), *The Secret Place*, *The Daily Bread*, and *Penned from the Heart*.

He has written three devotional books: *God's Help Now!* (out of print), *Devotions A-Z*, and *God's Divine Help;* and three fiction books, *Victim's Vengeance, Unveiled, and Jewel Time.*

Kenneth M. Lee
Loris SC 29569
E-mail: kenlwor@gmail.com

Preface

When I first got to Loris S.C., I began writing Bible devotions for the local newspaper.

That lasted for nearly ten years. Then I started a yearly booklet of devotions for distribution to funeral homes, help centers, restaurants, and homeless shelters. I did that for several years until I began to write fiction books.

Now, I've taken the devotions that were in the booklets and made this book *Southern Devotions*.

Many of the devotions are locally based --others are from the scriptures.

Regardless, the Lord was present.

Possibly, you have experienced such faith stories.

I hope you will write them down and share them with the public -- as a witness of God's presence.

Kenneth M. Lee, October 2023

The Need for God

A beautiful full moon was arcing high above the earth when I went outside to look at the weather before a one-hour trip to play golf with friends.

But a flow of warm air was drifting in from the ocean over this inland community, and it was mixing with cool temperatures to spread a thick fog.

I got in the car and prayed for safety – and then I chose to drive on a less traveled road to the golf course.

Thick fog lingered at the bog areas of the road, which limited my visibility, so I would slow down considerably despite a car that had suddenly come up behind me.

A few minutes later, the sun began to rise and it burned off some of the fog.

But not soon enough for a sports utility vehicle that was turned over on its side in a ditch just yards off the roadway.

The vehicle's interior light was still on – while a police car's flashing blue lights pierced the fog and gave an eerie glow to the whole scene.

I don't' know why the vehicle wrecked, but I do know God keeps us safe in times of danger.

Consider your activities for each day but also a God who has power over it all.

Many times in history when there was danger, famine, fear, or sickness, God was there to help his people. The people trusted in him for safety and prosperity, and they praised him at the end of the journey or completion of a job knowing it was he who should get the glory.

Nothing is more important in America today than for people turning to God for the right way to live. Like sheep, we may be astray -- but with God, there is safety knowing he is control.

And whatever ye do in word or deed, do all in the name of the Lord Jesus, giving thanks to God and the Father by him.

Colossians 3: 17

A Simple Witness

James McCoy is a junk man, and he'll admit it. He picks up junk at people's residences, drops some off at the recycling center, and sells some to a scrap metal yard.

He also sells some of it at his booth at the North Myrtle Beach flea market.

Humbly, he'll tell you he's not the smartest guy and doesn't read well.

But one day, after reading a simple scripture in the Book of St. John, he exclaimed, "I can understand this!"

That's what God does: he gives understanding and wisdom to a humble person.

James loves the Lord and is usually found playing gospel music at his booth on weekends. He sings aloud and invites anyone to look at his goods.

77 years young, he gives testimony to the goodness of God in a world of troubles.

Consider witnessing for God and Jesus like James does. We are not to be ashamed of the gospel (Romans 1:16).

Neither do we want to deny Jesus and be rejected by God (Matt. 10: 33).

And the angel of the Lord appeared unto the woman, and said unto her, Behold, now, thou art barren, and bearest not; but thou shalt conceive, and bear a son. Judges 13: 3

A Sacrificial Offering

There is a story in Judges Chapter 13 about an angel of the Lord appearing to a sterile woman and foretelling the birth of Samson -- who would be a ruler and judge over Israel for twenty years and free the people from Philistine oppression.

But before the woman would be blessed to conceive, she and husband Manoah were to offer a sacrifice to the Lord.

When they did, the angel of the Lord ascended into heaven, and the man and wife saw God.

"We are doomed to die!" Manoah said. "We have seen God!"

Consider that God is an awesome God who has power over life and death.

Here, a sacrificial offering was accepted by God, and the couple gave birth to Samson, who took out revenge on the Philistines.

Often, a fear of death gets in our way of serving God, but now we have Jesus as a sacrifice for death.

Death was defeated by Jesus when he arose from the grave, and he sits on the right hand of God for us.

Prayer: Lord, I thank you for Christ Jesus who is the sacrifice for my sin. Let me tell others about this wonderful gift from God. Amen.

He is the Rock, his work is perfect, for all his ways are justice; a God of truth and without iniquity, just and right is he. *Deut. 32: 4*

A Search for Truth

I went looking for truth one day at a library.

I found the library but I did not find truth – though I looked in many books that covered every religion in the world.

No. I found it in a dark sanctuary filled with the presence of God in sorrow, and there was nothing better than the experience.

Only Christianity could provide an answer for my spiritual hopelessness. The person of Jesus Christ, who came in the flesh and died for sin, completely redeemed me.

The Bible says, He is the propitiation for our sins and not for ours only, but also for the sin of the whole world (1 John 2: 2).

Neither are we to follow false doctrine (see Ephesians 4: 14 and Hebrews 13: 9)

We are to speak the truth in love, as Christ is the center of life.

Truth guides us to find God, and Jesus allows us to find truth.

The Biblical man David prayed: Unto thee, O Lord, do I lift up my soul: lead me in thy truth and teach me, for thou art the God of my salvation; on thee do I wait all the day (Psalms 25: 1-5).

This is my commandment, that ye love one another, as I have loved you.   *John 15: 12*

A Stranger in Christ

She had left home and travelled several hours to a quiet place near the ocean. When she arrived, she gathered her fishing gear and made her way downhill towards a pier, where I was fishing.

We exchanged nods, and after a few minutes, began to talk.

"My family is dying: my grandmother, grandfather, uncles, and a friend. I needed some time to get away."

I responded, "It's good to get away sometimes."

She was about 40 years old and rested her fishing pole against the pier railing. She set down a tackle box, spread out a canvas chair, which had a top on it for shade -- and sat back in the chair to bait her fishhooks with shrimp.

It was a clear day, and the tide was beginning to come in and lap the shoreline.

"You know Jesus?" I asked.

She said nothing but turned to me with her shirt showing lettering that said: *Faith is a Factor.*

I smiled and nodded.

Faith is a factor. It encourages us to do good work and witness about an almighty God who is in charge.

Consider faith, but also consider Jesus, who allows us to find God and faith.

The greatest faith we can have is to know God's Son Jesus died for our sins to give us salvation.

The Apostle Paul said: I live by the faith of the Son of God who loved me and gave himself for me (Galatians 2: 20).

The Lord is a man of war; the Lord is his name.
Ex. 15: 3

Fighting for God's Glory

There are multiple instances of men fighting for God's glory in the Bible, such as Joshua conquering foreign tribes to enter God's land of promise, David fighting a giant for victory over the Philistines; and Moses lifting his hands to defeat Amalek.

But fighting is vain without God's glory: there would be personal hurt, loss of material, and usually it takes weeks to recover.

And then we wonder why it happened.

The Bible gives us some wisdom: Strive not with a man without a cause, if he hath done thee no harm; do not envy the oppressor, and choose none of his ways (Proverbs 3: 30-31).

But if fighting occurs, make sure it's for God's glory, by the law of God.

Consider reading Deuteronomy Chapters 6-8 for a promise of victory.

Know also God's Son Jesus conquers inward fighting and gives us rest.

Jesus says, "Take my yoke upon you, and learn of me; for I am meek and lowly in heart, and ye shall find rest unto your souls" (Matthew 11: 29).

Rejoice evermore. Pray without ceasing. In everything, give thanks; for this is the will of God in Christ Jesus concerning you.   *1 Th. 5: 15-18*

Prayer

Yes, I will pray and I will pray, not ceasing, bowing my head to pray

Smiling each day while lifting prayer to God as I travel throughout the day

Sometimes softly saying Lord God to your precious name

Occasionally teary eyed or with smiles but never the same

My feeling is different each time I kneel and pray

Not always the same story, but still praying each day

So much to say, but apprehensive that I would miss the chance

So I lift up my daily praise and then do a glorified dance

Waiting patiently on His acknowledgment, not knowing when that would be

In my heart I am certain that He will address my prayers you see

It's divine when all else fails that the Lord will stay

That's why everyday I bow my head and pray and I pray and I pray.   *Virginia Brown*

And a certain man was there, who had an infirmity thirty and eight years.   *John 5: 5*

The Healing Jesus

There was an impotent man in John 5: 1-16 who was waiting for healing waters to be stirred by an angel before entering them and becoming healed but another man stepped in the pool before him.

Jesus was there, and he saw the impotent man's problem and questioned his desire to get well: "Wilt thou be made well?"

The man complained about the crowded pool.

But Jesus said, "Rise. Take up thy bed and walk."

Jesus knew it was faith in God and not worldly rituals that heal.

And the man became well.

Consider the world's practices for healing but also Jesus Christ, the Son of God whose death on the cross takes away sins and allows people to find God's wholesomeness.

Jesus heals us of infirmities (Hebrews 7: 25-28); we must only trust him and have faith.

The prayer of faith shall save the sick, and the Lord shall raise him up; and if he have committed sins, they shall be forgiven him; James 5: 15.

Nor height, nor depth, nor any other creation, shall be able to separate us from the love of God, which is in Christ Jesus, our Lord.   Romans 8: 39

Intimacy with God

There are moments Jesus had with God that are without comparison; such as Jesus being in God's temple with doctors of the law and interpreting scripture as a young child; being in a desert resisting evil temptations by quoting God's word; and having intimate prayers with God before death.

And Jesus was sure of each action.

Nothing else mattered to him because he was in total agreement with God almighty.

And that's the way it should be, because God is our creator and final authority.

Sacred moments with God are moments to remember, especially in times of trouble, persecution, or sickness. Thinking back on such moments gives confirmation that God is real and was in control.

The holiness of God through the sacrificial blood of Christ comforts, protects, and guides us through life to witness and share God's word along with achieving good works.

Consider also reading the Book of Isaiah, Chapters 56-58, for an intimate moment with God.

. . . Greater is he that is in you, than he that is in the world.

1 John 4: 4

A New Day in God's Hope

In the morning bright and glowing
Dawns the sun to bless the day,
Strews its beam, a joyous sewing,
Shades of night soon fade away.

Such a glorious inner splendor
Will dawn sweetly on that heart
Which with thoughts of worship tender
Early draws with God apart.

On the soul's horizon truly
Storms may come and bitter night,
But with rays of hope born newly,
We march on with growing might.

And in fact there is no other
Such a light with healing ray,
Which can free from hate our brother,
Save the world in darkest day.

So take hope, O Soul, awaken!
Shed more sunshine got through prayer
And this world, though God forsaken,
Will once more grow sweet and fair!

H. Habel

Let my people go, that they may hold a feast to me in the wilderness.   *Exodus 5: 1*

God in the Wilderness

God wanted his people to be free from Egyptian slavery, so he led them out of a camp of forced labor into a wilderness of freedom.

But there were dangers in the wilderness, and the people lacked water and food at times.

The people cried out to the Lord, and he provided them with water from a rock and manna from heaven.

Centuries later, God's Son Jesus was in a wilderness; and he too looked to God for help, for the devil was tempting Jesus with different choices. Jesus quoted God's word, and the devil left.

At the far western end of North Carolina, there is a forest untouched by loggers, hikers, or rock hounds (gem hunters). It's a true wilderness and quite an amazing sight to see if you appreciate natural beauty. But if you expect to see clean cut trees, smooth walking paths, and a blue sky peeking through the tall hemlocks, you'll be disappointed. This is a forest with decomposed tree limbs and trunks overlapping each other with musty bark residue.

But God is there -- just as he is here -- in town, home, or church. And in the wilderness, where there is often darkness and confusion, he still gives us comfort and guidance when we call on him.

Exhort one another, and so much the more, as ye see the day approaching.   Heb. 10: 25

The Inspirational Man

Encouraging one another should be a part of our daily activities, and years ago, I met a person who set a fine example.

I was performing a chore at work when another worker said, "Anyone can do that."

In other words, he was inspiring me to do better.

Willie McPherson, who worked beside me at the Norfolk Post Office forty years ago, was a person I looked to from then on.

He and I broke color barriers at work and play before they were made.

Mac died at 44 years old, but Ill never forget his passion for friendship, workers' rights, and integrity: he was also a union steward who cared about the employees.

Mentors come and mentors go, but consider Jesus, who sat with the poor, befriended strangers, and encouraged people.

He was compassionate in a world without hope, and his love for humanity continues today.

And Jesus increased in wisdom and stature, and in favor with God and man.   *Luke 2: 52*

A Child's Work

Arising at 5: 00 every morning and bicycling a mile to a street corner to fold and rubber band newspapers for delivery was rewarding at the end of the week by collecting monies from customers.

But consider Jesus, who as a child was sitting in a temple learning about God and talking with doctors of the law; (Luke 2: 49).

"Knew ye not that I must be about my Father's business?" he told his parents when they came looking for him.

But Jesus did have work to do at home: farming, cleaning, and maintaining shelter and land were necessary chores.

And so he went home and was subject unto them . . . (Luke 2: 51).

Jesus gives us a good example of a child being obedient to be his parents.

For as the heaven is higher than the earth, so are my ways higher than your ways, and my thoughts than your thoughts. Isaiah 55: 9

God's Mercy Above

Franz Sigler was a W.W. II German Air Force Pilot ace who flew 487 combat missions and had 30 victories over enemy planes earning a Knight's Cross.

Caught between suffering from "The Party" of Premier Adolf Hitler as a civilian or piloting German aircraft, he joined the Air Force but kept a rosary and Bible with him always.

One afternoon, while on a combat mission and coming upon a badly damaged B-17 bomber in the sky with a hole in its side, two faulty engines, and a flailed rudder with wounded crewmen, Franz backed off the final gun trigger and stared -- citing a higher call -- while looking at the wounded pilot Charlie Brown managing the yoke of the diving aircraft (*A. Makos, New York, 2012*).

If everyone had the "higher call" and an understanding of God's mercy, it would be a wonderful world.

Possibly, Franz had in mind the scripture: Glory be to God in the highest, and on earth peace; good will toward men (Luke 2: 14).

But he had lost a brother in the war, who was also a pilot.

Franz would later meet Charlie at a gathering of pilots of World War II years later, and many of their questions about that day would be answered.

The kingdom of God cometh not with observation. Neither shall they say, Lo here! Or, lo there! For, behold, the kingdom of God is in the midst of you.   Luke 17: 20-21

The Sign from Jesus

A day before Hurricane Matthew in North Carolina, I was sitting on a fishing pier bench looking at a blue sky with few clouds that resembled anything but hurricane driven.

But right before me was high water lapping against concrete pilings 3' foot above its normal height.

In other words, the most obvious sign of bad weather was right in front of me.

The Son of God said in a parable in Luke 11: 29 about people looking for a sign for the end of the world – but there would be none – except the sign of Jonah the Prophet, which signified God's judgment over the wicked people of Nineveh.

Jesus said in Luke 11: 32, "But now a greater than Jonah is here."

The righteous Jesus brings judgment.

Consider danger signs in the environment but also Jesus, who provides salvation and peace.

His resurrection from the grave gives us hope, as we worship him.

Give unto the Lord the glory due unto his name;
worship the Lord in the beauty of holiness.   Psalms 29: 2

Worshipping God

In the Appalachian Mountains there was a small group of people who met Sunday mornings and Wednesday evenings in a little brick church building at the foot of Soco Mountain.

On cold and wet mornings, the wood stove would have to be fired up with kindling, loose bark cleaned off the floor, sidewalk cleared of snow, and towels placed at the front entrance foyer to absorb the dripping water from people's shoes.

There might be sunlight shining through the crucifix stained glass windows if not so low in the winter and trying to find its way through a gap in the mountains, but more often than not, depending on the time of the year, its rays slept far into the morning and the windows remained frosted while parishioners exhaled steam.

Yet the sweet music from a solitary figure with a guitar filled the room -- as she chose to keep her talent in the church.

Consider your worship of God in the world.

Know also that Jesus says God is a spirit, and we are to worship him in spirit and truth.

God be merciful to me a sinner.

Luke 18: 13

The Justified Sinner

In the Book of Luke, Chapter 18: 10-14, there is a story about two men going to pray at a temple.

One man thanks God he is not like other men, who are described as unjust, adulterers, and extortionists – but the other man was ashamed in front of God and pleaded for mercy as a sinner.

Jesus said, "I tell you this man [the latter] went down to his house justified rather than the other."

God loves humility.

The mercy seat of forgiveness extends far into the realm of God's understanding when a person is remorseful about personal sin.

Dear Lord, I confess my sins and abandon them. I thank you for Christ who took my sins upon his back to the cross of death. Forgiveness is truly with you, and your mercy endures forever. Amen.

And the Spirit of God moved upon the face of the waters.   *Genesis 1: 2*

When God Moves

God can be very quiet sometimes, but when he moves, it's with purpose, like when he created the earth.

The Spirit of God can also move compassionately upon humans, like when he heard complaints of the Israelites and Moses and some elders to free people from slavery (see Exodus 3: 7-8).

But consider when God showed his power over the devil, who had afflicted the man Job with much suffering.

Satan was defeated, and Job regained his health -- and all that he had lost – because of God's presence.

God also moves prophetically, and that's why several books in the Bible are devoted strictly to prophecy.

In one instance, God wanted to get work done in a temple, so he stirred up the spirits to get it done! (Haggai 1: 14.)

But the best movement from God is when he sent his Son Jesus to earth to die for our sins.

We, then, as workers together with him, beseech you also that ye receive not the grace of God in vain.

2 Cor. 6: 1

The Value of Work

Why not quiet your idle dreaming
And get quickly to your work?
Take your task in hand this minute,
Never for a moment shirk,
And you'll find that with the effort
Flashes up a potent charm,
In the strength of which you'll master
What has lain beyond your arm.

There are heights which you may vision
From the ground where now you stand.
March right on! When that's ascended –
Greater heights will yet expand.
Yes, you'll have a weary struggle
And a fight to make the grade,
But take courage and remember
By sore trial the great are made.

Once you're on the road beginning
What you've set to be your goal.
Have no fears when storms beat 'round you;
You'll grow tall and strong and whole.

Henry Habel

And Adam called his wife's name Eve, because she was the mother of all living.   *Gen. 3: 2*

Mother of all Living

"Eve" also means "life giver", and without Eve, there would be no life because women would bear no children.

The word "Eve" was pronounced "em" in the Hebrew language, "me'ter" in the Greek, and is used 220 times in Biblical Hebrew.

Some of the more popular scriptures about mothers are: Honor thy father and mother, that thy days may be long upon the land . . . (Exodus 20: 12) -- and my favorite: Abandon not the law of thy mother (Proverbs 6: 20).

But mothers cannot be everywhere when needed.

We are reminded that a young man is to leave his father and mother – and cling unto his wife (Gen. 2: 24).

And Jesus says that no man has left father or mother but for his sake and the gospel: he will receive a hundredfold of fathers and mothers (Mark 10: 29).

And God said, Let us make man in our image.
Gen. 1: 26

The Trinity

The term *trinity*, which basically means *three*, weaved its way into theological literature by the early fathers of the Latin Church. It figuratively represents the Father, Son, and the Holy Spirit.

But the word "trinity" is not in the Bible, albeit the paradigm of 1 John 5: 7 where "three are agreed in one." (And this phrase was inserted by a copyist after the 14th century: it was not in the early original manuscripts according to Vine's Expository of Biblical words.)

The Sunday after Pentecost (the fiftieth day after Passover and the celebration of the descent of the Holy Spirit upon the Apostles) is called Trinity Sunday.

But consider the trinity designation.

The Godhead means different things to many people, but one thing is certain, God is still on the throne and the Holy Spirit awaits anyone that confesses Christ as Savior.

Then they led Jesus from Caiaphas to the hall of judgment, and it was early . . .   John 18: 28

The Power of Jesus

Jesus was being led to the governor of Judea, Pilate, for crucifixion.

But Pilate tried to get out of judging and condemning Jesus: it was the Jews who were bringing Jesus to this court because they said it was against their law to put a man to death.

Pilate found no fault in Jesus.

It amazes me how a person of little stature like Jesus had great power, and he showed this when Pilate threatened to crucify him.

Jesus said, "Thou couldest have no power at all against me, except it were given thee from above . . ." (John 19: 11).

Consider Jesus, though small in stature, became the greatest teacher and Savior on earth, because of God who had appointed him.

In the beginning was the Word, and the Word was with God, and the Word was God.   *John 1: 1*

The Simple Word

One of the most influential books of all time for finding peace is *Peace with God*, by the late Reverend Billy Graham.

Simply written, without prose, and eloquently presented, it has been instrumental in bringing people to know God's comfort through Jesus Christ.

The same might be said of the Book of St. John in the Bible: it is simple to read, and much of it in the present tense.

"Let not your heart be troubled; ye believe in God, believe also in me," Jesus said in Chapter 14: 1. (The author John was one of Christ's twelve disciples.)

When life seems confusing and unsure, consider turning to the simple word of God for comfort and truth.

The word of God is simple, and designed to help a person find truth, salvation from sin, and peace.

And there arose a great storm of wind, and the waves beat into the boat, so that it was now full.   Mark 4: 37

Peace and Security

Jesus was asleep at the stern of a boat when a big storm came along and scared his disciples enough to wake him and complain about the big waves.

"Teacher! Does it matter to you that we are perishing?" they said.

It appears the disciples were looking for sympathy and attention – rather than for ways to stabilize the boat and survive the storm.

But consider the storms of life – and how overwhelming they can seem at times.

If only we turn to Jesus, who sits at the right hand side of God, we can have peace.

Jesus rebuked the wind and the disciples with words of guidance: "Silence. Be still."

And there was a great calm.

And I will walk among you, and be your God; and ye shall be my people.   *Lev. 26: 12*

Travelling the Rocky Road

Anyone who has walked through rough country for miles not knowing if food or shelter will be available at the end of the day knows every step is precious around brush, large rocks, and puddles of water to save strength.

Stepping carefully to prevent damage to clothing and the body goes a long way towards getting to a good destination.

Consider the journey of the Hebrew children through the wilderness -- where there were hundreds of miles of rough terrain, poisonous insects, and enemies.

Some people arrived safely in God's land of milk and honey -- but others did not -- because of their unbelief and stubbornness to be led by a righteous God.

The history of Israel's travel to the land of God's promise is in Psalm 78.

Consider also Jesus, the Son of God, who takes away darkness to help us find the right path for life (Ephesians 5: 8-21).

Riches and honor are with me; yea durable riches and righteousness.   *Prov. 8:18*

The Precious Gem

After Bill got off from work every Friday, he packed his truck with picks and chisels and travelled a few hours south to the Georgia Mountains to hunt for gemstones such as rubies, garnets, and gold.

He sifted through the dirt from the sides of mountains and streams, and to Bill, it was a hobby.

But to many people, searching for gemstones and precious metals is a way to become worldly rich.

Never mind the sacrifices involved, of leaving family, material costs, or health problems.

There is a warning in Proverbs 8 that God's wisdom is better than rubies (Prov. 8: 11); his fruit is better than gold, yea, fine gold, and revenue is better than choice silver (Prov. 8: 19).

Consider the presence of God, who after jewels tarnish, dim, and lose their luster, provides comfort and peace.

Know also that God's Son Jesus is more precious than all the gemstones because of his power to save the soul upon confession of sin.

The Bible says we are not to think of the Godhead as gold, or silver, or man's device, but it is the precious blood of Jesus that has redeemed us from sin to give us salvation and life (Acts 17: 29; 1 Peter 1: 18-25).

And he opened his mouth and taught them, saying . . . .
Matt. 5: 1

The Great Sermon

The great Sermon on the Mount is in the Book of Matthew, Chapters 5-7.

It begins with, "Blessed are the poor in spirit; for theirs is the kingdom of heaven," (Matthew 5: 3).

What a great introduction! Because Jesus got the people's' attention quickly by identifying with their poverty and emotions.

The Book of Luke 6: 20-49 lists a similar sermon by Jesus, but this one takes place on a plateau. Multitudes of people came to hear him, for some were sick and vexed with unclean spirits.

Consider these sermons by Jesus and the people going home filled with the word of God and hope.

That's what Jesus does for anyone who accepts his words: "The words that I speak unto you, they are spirit, and they are life," (John 6: 63).

The words are especially powerful in Matthew 5: 3-12 about how to receive blessings, with nine examples.

Grace to you, and peace, from God, our Father, and from the Lord Jesus Christ.   *1 Cor. 1: 3*

The Greeting Word

A similar greeting was given to me every morning when I was delivering mail to a small white boarded house on my mail route.

A kind old gentleman would be sitting on a weathered couch on the front porch reading his Bible and waving at me.

"Praise the Lord!" he would exclaim when I was putting mail in his mail box.

He was disabled but still praising God from that couch.

And so we began a friendship, until one day, he wasn't there – he had passed on into God's kingdom.

Everyday I looked forward to discussing the Bible with him in those brief moments: it encouraged me throughout the day.

Consider your greeting to another person and an opportunity to present God as a blessing.

It may be that you will find a friend who knows God.

And they heard the voice of the Lord God walking in the cool of the day . . . .   *Genesis 3: 8*

The First Trial

The first court trial for people was in the Garden of Eden and four people were present: Adam, Eve, a devil serpent, and God.

There was a crime about Adam and Eve eating from the tree of knowledge of good and evil, from which God had told them not to eat. The serpent was a prime suspect of causing the forbidden fruit to be eaten.

God began to interrogate each person. He asked Adam, "Hast thou eaten of the tree, whereof I commanded thee that thou shouldest not eat?" And to the woman, he asked, "What is this that thou hast done?"

It was a pithy scene with Adam covering himself and Eve blaming the serpent.

But with God as prosecutor, judgment was pronounced and an order was given to all parties including expulsion from the Garden of Eden.

The serpent, which had deceived the woman into eating from the tree, was immediately cursed.

Trials come along in life that test our faith, correct our transgressions, and give us direction. But if we know God, we are only to be obedient to the first order to forego such trials.

And there was no water for the congregation; and they gathered themselves together against Moses and against Aaron.   *Numbers 20: 2*

The Fallen Priest

Aaron the priest was put to shame in front of the people in the Book of Numbers, Chapter 20, because he did not believe God could provide water out of a rock.

He and his companion Moses rebelled against God in this story at the waters of Meribah (Numbers 20: 7-13).

The Lord provided water from the rock but Moses and Aaron took credit for the miracle after they had beat against the rock with a rod.

As a result, not only did Aaron lose his priesthood when God ordered his garments be given to his son Eleazar– but he lost his life when God issued a decree (Numbers 20: 24-26).

Consider the infallibility of Aaron, who had seen God's glory at Mount Sinai but received God's harsh judgment for self-glory.

No one escapes judgment from God.

But also consider God's Son Jesus.

He was made a priest on earth with a crown of thorns and sits on the right hand side of God to intercede and give life everlasting.

Looking to Jesus, the author and finisher of faith, who for the joy that was before him endured the cross, despising the shame, and is set down at the right hand of the throne of God.   Heb. 12: 2

Strangers upon Earth

People in the Bible have proclaimed to be strangers upon earth after meeting God face to face and receiving eternal salvation and redemption of sin.

And so they proclaimed God's throne as their real home.

The author of The Epistle to the Hebrews says: But now they desire a better country, that is, a heavenly . . . for he hath prepared for them a city; Hebrews 11: 16.

A home and city with peace, joy, fellowship, and trust! How wonderful that would be!

This reminds me of being in a foreign country where the language is confusing, street signs have oblique names, road rules are different, and there's some bigotry among the people -- it's not home.

But regardless of where we're at, God is still our caretaker and landlord.

Come now, therefore, and I will send thee to Pharaoh, that thou mayest bring forth my people, the children of Israel, out of Egypt.   Ex. 3: 10

The Moses Place

Moses was a rancher when God came along and gave him a job to help his people escape slavery.

Once Moses assumed the job as leader, there's little doubt he used his farm experience to help, feed, teach, and shelter the people.

But more important, he taught them to worship God -- and the people built altars throughout their journeys.

Moses never left the place of God's calling, though the people warred, hungered, and worshipped idols at times. Moses stayed the course to complete the mission.

But he wasn't without temptations and troubles.

One time he ran away from a rod of power that God had given him when it turned into a serpent (Exodus 4: 1-4). Scared and intimidated, he turned back to God, listened to him for instruction, and caught the serpent with God's presence.

Consider the faith of Moses who loved God and always returned to him for guidance.

We are also called to perform missions, but nothing should lead us astray from a God who is always present.

And the men of Judah said, "Why are ye come up against us?" And they answered, "To bind Samson are we come up, to do to him as he hath done to us." Judges 15: 10

Samson's Vengeance

A former ruler of Israel named Samson was captured by the Philistines and chained.

He was put in a prison house, forced to turn a millstone wheel to grind grain into flour in the Book of Judges, Chapter 16, and had his eyes put out and hands bound.

But the Spirit of God was still present.

When the Philistines sported him before a crowd of people in an arena, Samson wanted vengeance.

So he talked the guard into moving him between two main support columns of the arena. He said a prayer and pulled the columns down, much to the detriment of thousands of people who fell to their deaths.

The Bible says God avenges his elect (Deut. 32: 43).

Consider the words of Jesus in Luke 18: 3: "I tell you that he will avenge them [the elect of God] speedily. Nevertheless, when the Son of man cometh, shall he find faith on the earth?"

When thou passest through the waters, I will be with thee.   *Isaiah 43: 2*

Safe Passage

    I was on my way to Germany in a C-130 aircraft for an allied training exercise.

    The seats were no more than 18" wide and made of cargo web strapping enclosed by riveted metal panels lined up and down the aisles of the aircraft.

    It was dark – with only an ember light of a cigarette from a nervous soldier's hand arcing back and forth from his mouth -- in anticipation of a possible drowning I suppose.

    The craft was flying under radar at 500 foot above sea level over the cold choppy waters of the Atlantic Ocean.

    I shifted my M-16 rifle regaining my sleep posture and prayed for God's safety as the plane jolted a few times and I heard a banging sound from the bottom of the plane, which I assumed to be the landing gear. I didn't know whether to be happy or worried.

    Some trips are scary.

    Consider troubles in life's journey but also God before, during, and after.

    God comforts us in all activities, when we read scripture and pray towards his holy temple.

But whoso hearkeneth unto me shall dwell safely, and shall be quiet from fear of evil.

Proverbs 1:33

When God Passes By

I went up to a store one day to buy some goods when I noticed the cashier was nervous after she dropped a few things before she could scan them.

I asked her what was wrong, and she said she had just been in an accident.

I didn't want do delve much further into her privacy, so I said, "I'll be right back."

And I went to my car to retrieve a devotional book that I knew could help her regardless of the problem.

I stopped by the store again in a couple days and she thanked me for the book -- said it came at the just the right time.

God's word helps us at the right time -- whether by book, person, or divine presence. It shows God is in control. And we know he has compassion and understanding.

But we should not wait for God to pass by.

Know that he is available to anyone who calls on His name and bows in humble adoration.

Being justified freely by his grace through the redemption that is in Christ Jesus.   *Romans 3: 24*

Redemption

God is the God of redemption and mercy I found out one night after visiting my father and laying my head on his frail chest asking forgiveness for arguing with him years earlier.

"Forgiveness should be an everyday part of our lives, shouldn't it?" he replied.

I nodded my head unable to speak – and I wept -- not fully understanding mercy at the time.

But redemption is what I got that night, because two hours later I got a phone call saying he had died.

My brother was not as fortunate: he was not humble enough to visit our father. As a result, he suffered the rest of his life.

Consider redemption – the act of becoming free from guilt and grief. Though not always available from people, the Bible says of Christ: In whom we have redemption through his blood, the forgiveness of sins, according to the riches of his grace (Ephesians 1: 7).

Consider your redemptive process but also Jesus as redeemer (1 Peter 1: 13-25): that your faith and hope be in God who raised up Jesus from the dead and gave him glory.

*Arise, go to Nineveh, that great city, and cry against it;
for their wickedness is come up against me.*

Jonah 1: 2

The Mission of Jonah

The Biblical character Jonah had a mission to go to the city of Nineveh and pronounce God's judgment but instead, he boarded a boat to Tarshish.

A storm arose and the boat was about to break apart. The mariners became scared, and they knew God was behind their destruction because Jonah had told them about his foregone mission.

Jonah was interrogated and found guilty of neglecting God's mission to go to Nineveh. His conscience was convicted, and he said he would rather be thrown overboard to save the boat and its crew from destruction.

Jonah got his wish to be thrown overboard, but he never escaped his original mission to go to Nineveh!

Jonah was swallowed by a great fish but spit out upon dry land, to resume the journey.

Serving God is not always a happy venture, but it's better than suffering like Johan did.

In all labor there is profit, but the talk of the lips tendeth to penury (destitution or poverty). Proverbs 14: 23

Profitable Labor

It was an older Cape Cod style house that had a steep A-frame roof that leaked water and I'd have to go up into the attic to get it stopped.

It was a good reason to pull the ceiling chain and climb a ladder, but the old pots that were filled from the previous rainstorm would have to be carried back down and emptied.

Then I'd go back up in the attic with the empty pots and look above at the wooden knotty pine roof planks trying to find the new dripping leaks. I'd place the pots on the ceiling carefully under the falling water.

It wasn't a big job, but years later I'd find myself fixing roofs to make a living; so I valued the experience.

We are created by God to do good works.

In contrast, a lazy person will suffer to be hungry (see Proverbs 19: 15).

Consider work in life -- that despite a lack of knowledge to do something, God still wants us to labor in some small way to make things better.

Know also Jesus, the greatest worker of all, who by faith healed people and worked for God to spread a message of truth and love.

For thou art my hope, O Lord, God, thou art my trust from my youth. *Psalms 71: 5*

Prayer for Old Age

The fire was intense, *but locust wood burns hot,* I thought as I looked at the flickering flames and sparks flying in the wood stove. *The stove would still need an oak log to make it last through this cold winter night however.*

So I turned around, opened the side door, and stepped onto the snow-dusted ground to retrieve a log from under the woodpile cover. I hurriedly got back in the cabin to escape a howling wind and I threw the log in the stove. I closed the stove door and opened the draft screws slightly to allow more airflow. And I sat down nearby.

Everyone was gone. The kids were gone. There was no laughter and no one to fix breakfast for the next day. A half-moon became visible through the cracks in the logs.

This was my situation in the middle of winter of 1994; yet I was blessed with a little food, money, and some humble native friends who loved the Lord.

Consider the brevity of life. The Book of James says it is as a vapor that appears for a little while, then vanishes (James 4: 14). The years pass by quickly.

Fortunately, God has provided the Bible for a guide.

If you don't know God's presence, consider reading scriptures or visiting a local church.

Regardless of whatever situation you are in, true happiness is only a prayer away in Christ.

For the joy of the Lord is your strength . . . .
Nehemiah 8: 10

Nehemiah's Work and Joy

The phrase "the joy of the Lord is your strength" is often heard in a church service.

But the phrase has a different meaning in the original Hebrew. It goes like this: *The joy of Jehovah is your fortress.*

And that makes sense, because Nehemiah and company were building a wall around Jerusalem under threats.

After finishing the wall, they would celebrate Jehovah's guidance and protection with a feast and reading of the law to the congregation of people (see Nehemiah Chapter 8).

We should diligently search the scriptures for understanding (Deut. 6: 9; 1 Peter 2: 2); otherwise, we may be missing the true meaning of a story or scripture.

Consider the joy that comes from a job well done, but also know that God's Son Jesus allows us to break down a wall of sin.

He came to give us joy by taking our sins to the cross of death.

The earth is the Lord's, and the fullness thereof; the world, and they who dwell therein.   *Psalms 24: 1*

God's Work in Nature

A new person on a fire fighting team usually gets the unenviable task of carrying a chainsaw, tools, or medical equipment on walks through charred remains of fallen tree limbs, thick brush, or smoke filled roads.

I was on a team many years ago. While walking up a steep incline on an old logger's road bordered by a gulley with a thick bed of dry leaves, I heard a rushing air sound behind me -- a vacuum type sound, and I looked back to the left fifty feet to see fire engulfing the depression of earth I had just passed.

God's actions in nature are awesome.

Consider that we are small creatures on earth and within a large universe; yet God cares enough about us to look down and visit with mercy (Psalms 8).

For he hath founded it upon the seas, and established it upon the floods. Who shall ascend into the hill of the Lord? Or who shall stand in his holy place? (Psalms 24: 1-3).

The psalmist David says there is only one way to stand in the holy place, He who hath clean hands, and a pure heart, who hath not lifted up his soul unto vanity, nor sworn deceitfully ((Psalms 24: 4).

Now we have Jesus, who takes away sin and renews us to live clean and humble lives.

Seek the Lord while he may be found, call ye upon him while he is near.   *Isaiah 55: 6*

God's Presence Today

You may walk with God in the Garden;
Feel His touch on your bed of pain.
Sense Him near in the counsel needed
Thrill to hear of His Holy name
But you're only still on the border
Of where God would have you to be
To live your life in His Presence
In a daily happy degree
He would be to you as your breathing
Apart, yet in you as a whole
Where heaven is all round about you,
In filling the depth of your soul
When His pulse with yours beats to rhythm
What marvel shall man come to see
God walking the earth in your person
What a glory when that comes to be
For once you are part of His Being
You become His Garden of Prayer
You are seen as the touch of His healing
His counsel, His aid, and His care
Where you live, He lives in your serving
God's Way will be found in your walk
And in your loving persuasion
Men often shall hear their God talk
Quite soon will be found in your sowing
Of all God's heavenly seed
A harvest of children, home going
God's Family, with you in the lead

Henry Habel

Ye cannot serve God and money
Matt. 6: 24

God or Money

God never takes a back seat to a desire for money, and he warns us in the 1st Commandment about not bowing down before any other god: *Thou shalt have no other gods before me.*

Jesus shows us why God should be our first priority for life: "Lay not up for yourselves treasures upon earth, where moth and rust doth corrupt, and where thieves break through and steal. But lay up for yourselves treasures in heaven . . . "(Matt. 6: 20).

Heaven is where we want to spend our time, because it is idyllic, peaceful, and near God.

But a desire for money that is covetous will lead to worry, fear, and disappointment.

People have gone to great trouble to accumulate lots of money, only to end up in great trouble. Jacob deceived his father to get his brother's birthright inheritance and had to run away for years. Joseph's brothers' tried selling Joseph into slavery only to end up starving. And probably the most renown story is when the disciple Judas sold information about Jesus for thirty pieces of silver and hung himself.

True riches are with Christ Jesus who rose into heaven and intercedes for us to give prosperity (Ephesians 1: 7-14).

Thy faithfulness is to all generations; thou hast established the earth, and it abideth.   Psalms 119: 90

The Old Metal Pipe

There's an old metal pipe about five foot long sticking out from a crevice of rocks on the north side of a hill back at the old home place in the mountains.

Out of the pipe flows fresh water, which, depending on rainfall, fills an old washtub beneath it in an hour or so -- or it may take several days to fill the tub when the water barely drips.

But the area around the washtub needs maintenance on occasion: fallen leaves need cleared, the pipe may need reamed out, and the path to it freed of downed tree limbs, rattler snakes, and mud holes.

We need such maintenance to live God's word. Our thoughts should be clear, food diet should be pleasing (Romans 14), and our lives free of clutter that prevents us from worshipping God.

Reading the Word, witnessing Jesus, and praying without ceasing are good habits to have each day for maintenance.

Forever, O Lord, thy word is settled in heaven. Thy faithfulness is unto all generations; that thou established the earth, and it abideth forever (Psalms 119: 89-90).

And as they thus spoke, Jesus himself stood in the midst of them, and saith unto them, Peace be unto you.
Luke 24: 36

Meeting Jesus

Meeting Jesus is like coming out of a dark canyon where boulders have fallen, dust is swirling, and the exit is blocked with a large rain cloud approaching over the ridge that looks like it's going to pour at any minute.

Just as life seems hopeless and there's nowhere to turn for help, Jesus seems to manifest himself.

That's the promise in John 14: 23, where he and the Father will come into a person's life. "If a man love me, he will keep my words; and my Father will love him, and we will come unto him, and make our abode with him."

This is a mystery.

It's such a mystery that many people have sought to disprove the manifestation of Jesus -- only to come face to face with the living Christ.

The disciple Thomas had trouble believing until he saw the wounds from the crucifixion.

Jesus saith unto him: "Thomas, because thou hast seen me, thou hast believed; blessed are they that have not seen, and yet have believed" (John 20: 29).

Consider learning about Jesus *before* needing Jesus.

Bless ye the Lord, all ye his hosts, ye ministers of his, that do his pleasure.   *Psalms 103: 21*

Minister of the Word

Sergeant Blackerby was a chaplain in my artillery unit in Korea in 1973.

A simple looking man with wire rimmed glasses, flat gray hair, and dressed out in a starched green uniform with shiny polished black boots – there he would be in front of gun-toting, unshaven dirty soldiers at Sunday services on mud swathed fields with his Bible to give comfort to depressed and lonely men.

In some cases, it was their only hope.

God has installed priests, chaplains, and ministers to provide spiritual care for people who are lost, confused, or depressed.

The Apostle Paul in Romans 10: 14, gives them inspiration to minister, "How shall they hear without a preacher?"

Consider this gift from God to communicate the word of life to other people.

But know also Jesus Christ, who is the great high priest, and who sits on the right hand side of God.

For such an high priest was fitting for us, who is holy, harmless, undefiled, separate from sinners, and made higher than the heavens (Heb. 7: 26).

Then Job answered and said, I have heard many such things. Miserable comforters are ye all.   Job 16: 2

Job's Three Friends

Eliphaz, Bildad, and Zophar have long been known as "comforters" to their friend Job who suffered loss of family, livestock, farm, and his health after being attacked by the devil.

But when Job couldn't get the answers he was looking for from his friends, he called them *miserable comforters.*

They couldn't have been to miserable. Each man, after hearing of Job's problem, left home, sat down with Job on the ground (seven days), wept, tore personal clothing (a sign of penitence), and sprinkled dust upon the head towards heaven (Job 2: 12).

And none spoke a word during that time, for they saw that Job's grief was great (Job 2: 13).

Looking upon senseless destruction of property and suffering can leave person speechless. .

Sensitive leader Eliphaz was the first to respond, and he carried on with a message of hope in Chapter 4.

As for Job, he cursed the day he was born (Job 3).

But consider these three friends and their dedication to God, speaking of him in great speeches.

They kept the Spirit alive through God by innocence, wisdom, and humility, which gave Job hope.

It is a good thing to give thanks to the Lord, and to sing praises to his name, O most high. To show forth thy loving kindness in the morning, and they faithfulness every night.

Psalms 92: 1-2

Quiet Faith

The bare living room floor would be freezing I thought as I lay in bed and heard grandma's feet shuffle slowly on the kitchen floor towards the sink.

The living room would be dark -- with sunlight yet to find its way through the tall hemlocks that filled the eastern mountain.

It was cold and I knew the heater needed wood; so I quietly exited the bedroom and glanced at the stove, which I knew to be harboring the last few coals of an oak log from the previous night. I made my way outside to get some dried kindling limbs off the porch.

But Grandma was in the kitchen -- and quietly put two bowls of hot oatmeal on the table. Without speaking, she donned her coat to go outside and start her own fire – for a day of stripping honeysuckle vines for weaving baskets and dyeing them with walnut shells.

Her quiet faith in God spoke through her work.

The Bible has many examples of quiet faith, but today, Grandma showed me hers.

Nevertheless, when he the Spirit of truth, is come, he will guide you into all truth; for he shall not speak of himself, but whatever he shall hear, that shall he speak, and he will show you things to come. John 16: 13

Inalienable Truths

There are inalienable truths in the world such as the sun rising in the east, the moon revolving around the planet, water covering most of the earth, and condensation occurring when hot meets cold.

But the Bible also contains inalienable truths about people: a man is a man, a woman is a woman, animals inhabit the earth, people have to work and eat; there is life and death, good and bad – and contrary to what many people think – people need a divine god in times of trouble (see Genesis 4: 26).

Opposing these principles is vain because they are inalienable truths.

But consider also an inalienable truth from Jesus in John 14: 6, "I am the way, the truth, and the life."

"Heaven and earth shall pass away but my words will not pass away," he also said, in Mark 13: 31.

And how right he was, because his word still stands as inalienable truth 2000 years later.

Behold, I send an angel before thee, to keep thee in the way, and to bring thee into the place which I have prepared.

Ex. 23: 20

Preparation

Harry Carson played football with the New York Giants for thirteen years and was inducted into the Hall of Fame as a defensive lineman.

He had grown up in Florence, South Carolina, went to college and graduated at South Carolina State University, and was drafted in the fifth round.

Harry was successful because he was always prepared: he wore shoulder pads for a game, ran miles for conditioning, and studied acclaimed lineman Bill Bergey's play.

But Harry never lost sight of the future after football – he continued schooling to become a business man and sports broadcaster.

Consider a worldly profession but also life thereafter -- when the body slows and the days dim.

Many people think the Book of Ecclesiastes, Chapter 12: 1-7, summarizes life's journey: Remember now thy Creator in the days of thy youth, then shall the dust return to the earth as it was, and the spirit shall return to God who gave it.

Know also that God's Son Jesus prepares us for life or death by confession of faith (John 14: 2).

"I will sing unto the Lord . . . the horse and his rider he hath thrown into the sea."   *Exodus 15: 1*

Triumphant Glory

There's nothing more exhilarating then scoring a winning touchdown playing football, hitting a ball for a game winning home run in baseball, or winning a legal case of monumental proportions in court.

No doubt the Biblical man Moses felt wonderful about seeing Pharaoh's army drown in a sea.

He was so excited he mentioned it three times in a song of redemption while his sister Miriam danced to the music and words.

But imagine the feeling of God's son Jesus having victory over the devil: "I have overcome the world" (John 16: 33).

And then he exclaimed to the penitent thief while hanging on the cross: "Today shalt thou be with me in paradise" (Luke 23: 43).

We can be so joyful. Victory over personal sin and the fear of death with Jesus are good reasons.

And he ran ahead, and climbed up into a sycamore tree to see him; for he was to pass that way.   *Luke 19: 4*

The Zaccheus Tree

Zaccheus got a good look at Jesus from the sycamore tree, and Jesus got a good look at Zaccheus.

He told Zaccheus: "Make haste, and come down; for today I must abide at thine house" (Luke 19: 5).

There was an obvious urgency in the words from Jesus.

For one thing, Jesus was being threatened by the authorities, and Zaccheus was a rich man who needed salvation.

Come down from the heights of self-glory!

And then God will bless us with Jesus who can take away sin.

God blesses us with Jesus who can take away sin.

We then become stewards and fellow citizens in the kingdom of God.

There's no greater honor.

Zaccheus joyfully received Jesus into his home and life.

Believe on the Lord Jesus Christ, and thou shalt be saved, and thy house.   *Acts 16: 31*

Believe

Christ's disciples were in prison because they were teaching God's word and the resurrection of Christ.

But the prison guard had fallen asleep, with the doors to the prison open, and when he awoke, he was scared to death knowing he would be severely disciplined.

But the disciples were still there and they encouraged him to believe on the Lord Jesus Christ to be saved.

The way you believe will either keep you bound in darkness or set you free.

If you are a superstitious person and believe you will have seven years of bad luck for breaking a mirror, then bad things will happen if you break a mirror.

But there is no such thing as luck with the Christian -- there is confidence -- that God will fulfill any petition asked of him.

We are blessed. We are not lucky.

Jeanette Cole

And Moses said unto the Lord, "O my Lord, I am not eloquent, neither heretofore nor since thou hast spoken unto thy servant; but I am slow of speech and of a slow tongue."

Ex. 4: 10

Sharing the Word

The great leader Moses had a talking problem, so God sent Aaron the priest to do some talking for him until one day, God helped Moses to speak eloquently.

That's what God does: he fixes things.

When we're not very good at one thing, we may need some help, but in time, he'll perfect that which was deficient.

Brother James admits he doesn't read very well, because he grew up on a farm, and had no time for reading.

But he can talk! And he learns a lot by talking to other people and sharing his faith.

As a result, he has many friends and gets many jobs when someone needs something done.

Now, after prayer and study, he can actually read good.

He's a prime example of using what God has given him to be successful.

Therefore, if any man be in Christ, he is a new creation; old things are passed away; behold, all things are become new.

2 Cor. 5: 17

Removing the Unwanted

My stepfather used to gather buckeye wood in the mountains and let it dry for a couple of months.

Then he cut off a chunk and started whittling any part that did not look like the figure he wanted. He made pelicans, bears, foxes, and a host of other animals.

How similar is that to a newborn person in Christ when God takes away the bad and leaves the good?

Consider the scriptures of Ephesians 4: 31-32: Let all bitterness, and wrath, and anger, and clamor, and evil speaking, be put away from you, with all malice; And be ye kind one to another, tenderhearted, forgiving one another, even as God, for Christ's sake, hath forgiven you.

The selfish traits are put away and the new ones in Christ take their place.

But this redemptive process takes time -- just as the woodcarver takes time to make his final shape.

God is faithful to complete the work he has begun.

Why do the nations rage and the peoples imagine a vain thing?   *Psalms 2: 1*

The Wrong Idea

Mankind has been warned not to develop ideas contrary to God's law in the first commandment: Do not make any image of God in the heavens above, on earth, or from under the earth (Exodus 20: 3-5).

In other words, don't conjure up any idea of God that doesn't conform to being holy.

There were men at Babel in the land of Shinar in Genesis Chapter 11 that conjured up an image to build a tower to heaven.

But God saw their work, and he came down from heaven to meet them and confound their language.

The Bible says, For I am the Lord who bringeth you up out of the land of Egypt, to be your God; ye shall therefore be holy, for I am holy (Lev 11: 45).

Purity, righteousness, and mercy are traits of God that we should enjoy upon confession of faith. We must only be humble and obedient to the scriptures to experience such gifts. .

The right place to start knowing God is by Jesus as a redeemer of sin. Upon forgiveness of sin, we are ready to serve the living God.

Jesus said, "All things that the Father hath are mine; therefore said I, that he shall take of mine, and shall show it unto you" (John16: 15).

I will say of the Lord, he is my refuge and my fortress, my God; in him will I trust.   Psalms 91: 2

The Shelter of God

A cool wind began to blow as I rounded a corner to a hill a few hundred yards away.

I was on a 500 mile bicycle trip to the Smoky Mountains and in the back country.

Dark clouds started to form, and I was wondering where I could find shelter from what looked like either a tornado or strong hail storm.

I saw a church up ahead, and there was a clapboard farmhouse in the background with a lone oak tree shading the yard. Both were welcome sights.

As the wind got stronger, I pedaled faster until I reached the door of the church.

I arrived just in time as rain and hail began to pelt the ground around me. The door was unlocked, so I lifted my bicycle up the steps into the foyer just as the storm got stronger.

Consider shelter on earth but also God giving us protection from life's storms.

The psalmist says, Surely he shall deliver thee from the snare of the fowler; and from the noisome pestilence (Psalms 91: 3).

He is as near to us as calling on his name for help in time of trouble.

Now Moses, in the law, commanded us that such should be stoned; but what sayest thou?   *John 8: 5*

The Silent Stone

Stoning a person in Biblical times was a disciplinary action taken by God's people to expel a person from a community or invoke capital punishment.

But the woman at the well in John 8 received mercy.

No doubt there were plenty of stones on the ground near the temple from the construction of the walls and pathways, but no one stoned her.

But Jesus had said, "He that is without sin among you, let him first cast a stone at her"; (John 8: 7).

Jesus knew everyone has sinned at one time or another, so he gave them permission to throw stones.

When the law can not free a person from the consequences of sin, Jesus can, because he took our sins to the cross of death.

And they who heard it, being convicted by their own conscience went out, one by one . . . (John 8: 9).

And hope maketh not ashamed, because the love of God is shed abroad in our hearts by the Holy Spirit who is given unto us. **Romans 5: 5**

Hope

The word "hope" has been made insignificant in our vocabulary -- it has become more like wishing.

"Well, I hope it works out", someone might say.

Or, "I'm hoping it will be okay."

But the definition of hope is to cherish a desire with anticipation – to trust.

I lived in hopelessness for so long it made me numb to living a life filled with happiness.

Ecclesiastes 9: 4 says, For to him that is joined to all the living there is hope; for a living dog is better than a dead lion.

When I read the book of Ecclesiastes while I was suffering depression, it made me laugh. A depressed person knows another depressed person wrote this book.

For some reason, God used this book of the Bible to show me that even King Solomon struggled with depression.

So I was not alone.

But there is hope in Christ Jesus, who was raised from the dead to give us life, when we believe.

Jeanette Cole

For as the rain cometh down, and the snow from heaven, and returneth not there but watereth the earth, and maketh it bring forth and bud . . . so shall my word be that goeth forth out of my mouth; it shall not return unto me void, but it shall accomplish that which I please . .
Isaiah 55: 10-11

The Enduring Word of God

The town of Whiteville N.C experienced heavy flooding from a hurricane several years ago that sent high water into shops and businesses located on both sides of Madison Ave.

One business owner said, "The water was up to the fourth step on my upstairs business."

But if there had been fewer obstructions in the waterways, the water may have easily exited to a nearby river.

Consider materials such as concrete, debris, or added dirt in pristine wetlands that restrict water flow -- but also hindrances to God's word.

Rulers jailed the Apostle Paul for preaching the gospel, but he carried on God's work and now his letters are contained in the Bible to give us encouragement.

The devil still tries to stop the good news of Jesus from being spread, but nothing can hinder God's word, as it still endures today.

But seek ye first the kingdom of God, and his righteousness, and all these things shall be added unto you.

Matt. 6: 33

Dependence on God

There was a single light bulb hanging from the ceiling along a drooping wire that gave off just enough warmth to dry the cool damp air coming from the dirt floor.

I stared at it for the longest time – thinking about how some countries like here in Korea, where I was stationed in 1973, do not have abundant electricity, or running water.

I shifted myself from a lone mattress and lowered myself to exit the small hooch to find a well for water.

The thought stayed with me: life does not consist of acquiring earthly possessions -- but to have treasures in heaven -- as Jesus taught.

Returning back to the small house, I had a joyous feeling of the spirit of God fulfilling my needs.

The Bible says, But my God shall supply all your need according o the riches in glory by Christ Jesus (Philippians 4: 19).

Consider luxuries in life that may be available but also Jesus, who depended on the Word of God for life; he carried neither money nor bread, yet God supplied him with necessities.

For all that is in the world, the lust of the flesh, and the lust of the eyes, and the pride of life, is not of the Father, but is of the world.   *1 John 2: 16*

The Ways of the World

My dad was a business man.

Along with selling refrigeration equipment, he managed restaurants, pest control operations, and was a clerk for a trucking company.

He also volunteered in the community -- leading a fraternal organization of young men -- and manning an emergency radio station for truck drivers who needed directions and information as they were driving to the Hampton Roads area of Virginia.

He was a good man.

But goodness does not get a person into the kingdom of heaven. We are to profess our faith in the living Christ and be obedient to God the Father.

Neither are we saved by works (James 2: 14-26).

As a result of dad living the ways of the world, he passed away at 56 years old.

Consider taking time to commune with God in a holy place. Know God is the true happiness for life, and that his presence is divine.

The world [will] pass away, and the lust of it, but he that doeth the will of God abideth forever (v. 17).

And let us consider one another to provoke unto love and to good works, not forsaking the assembling of ourselves together . . .   *Heb. 10: 25*

The Season of Worship

The Georgia Mountains are beautiful in autumn with lush green valleys, agriculture and livestock farms, and plant life that borders creeks and hillsides.

There is usually a Christian church or synagogue in every small town.

I visited a Catholic church in Monroe County one Thanksgiving week and listened to a priest talk about the gospel of Christ. The priest talked said believers should love all of humanity despite adversity and persecution.

"Set an example," he exhorted.

Jesus set an example of God's love when he visited the sick, ate with sinners, and told people about God's mercy and righteousness. He preached a new covenant of belief and freedom from the bondage of sin and fear of death – through the sacrifice of his blood – and resurrection into heaven.

The singing was glorious at the church.

Consider your place of worship this season.

By him, therefore, let us offer the sacrifice of praise to God continually, that is, the fruit of our lips giving thanks to his name (Hebrews 13: 15).

Be not rash with thy mouth, and let not thine heart be hasty to utter any thing before God; for God is in heaven, and thou upon earth, therefore let thy words be few.

Eccl. 5: 2

Heaven's Quest

The cashier said she had died and went to heaven.

She also said she saw her mother and father and some other relatives as she passed through the pearly gate.

This was her first day back to work after a sickness and using some leave time.

I nodded my head politely and mentioned she did well to come back after all she had been through.

A man named Enoch was translated into heaven in Genesis 5: 24, then nothing else is said about him.

But consider Elijah, who was taken up by a whirlwind into heaven *twice* in 2 Kings 2. Maybe "twice" had something to do with Elisha requesting a double portion of Elijah's spirit.

Don Piper, the preacher returning from a conference had a traffic accident and went to heaven. He said he saw angels singing and heard musical instruments.

Consider heaven's vision from earth but also Jesus, who rose into heaven after a third day of death and sat on the right side of God.

Jesus said, "Heaven and earth may pass away, but my words shall never pass", Luke 21: 33.

How wonderful to know that the words of Jesus stay with us despite our experiences!

Jesus is a Savior we can trust to help us whether on earth or in heaven.

Seek the Lord while he may be found, call ye upon him while hi is near.
Isaiah 55: 6

God Awaits

The aircraft screeched to a thundering halt with airless tires that had been previously shot out by authorities in Orlando, Florida.

The authorities were trying to prevent the plane from taking off in Orlando because there was a group of hijackers on board.

The pilot miraculously landed the plane with flat tires in Havana, Cuba.

Later, after this hi-jacking episode was over, Captain Haas sat silently criticizing himself for making decisions *on his own* to save 75 passengers.

"How could I be so stupid?" he asked himself. "Why didn't I ask the Lord to do it [end the hi-jacking ordeal] a little sooner?" (Blair, 1977, Odyssey of Terror).

The Bible says, Trust in the Lord with all thine heart, and lean not unto thine own understanding (Prov. 3: 5).

There are times to seek God's intervention and speak with God's authority.

But passengers later testified they survived the ordeal with lots of prayers.

And the seventy returned again with joy, saying, Lord, even the demons are subject unto us through thy name.
Luke 10: 17

Overjoyed

Joy is the feeling the disciples had after going into towns and healing people.

And Jesus was joyful.

The Bible says, In that hour Jesus rejoiced in the Spirit . . . (Luke 10: 21).

He gave full credit to the Lord for such great work.

Consider the joy that comes from completing a work project or good deed -- but also the joy of telling people about God, who gives peace and prosperity through the knowledge of the scriptures and Jesus Christ.

It was for joy that Jesus was born into the world.

Our sins are taken away and life can be lived to its fullest.

By humility and fear of the Lord are riches, and honor, and life.   *Proverbs 22: 4*

Abraham's Humility

Humility is a great trait to have in front of God, and the biblical patriarch Abraham gives a good example.

While sitting in front of his tent on a hot day, he met three men and immediately went about the task of preparing food for them (Genesis 18).

He was also humble when letting nephew Lot choose some grazing land for a herd of animals (Genesis 13).

And he was humble when dealing with a foreign king in Genesis 20.

Yet Abraham could also be a man of war, a traveler, and builder of altars for God.

Because of his knowledge of God's ways, he was made rich with gold and livestock -- and blessed with a family.

It takes humility, patience, and obedience to receive blessings.

Humility is often learned by suffering. Abraham, who was at one time starved for food, had to travel many miles to receive help (Genesis 12).

He had to depend on God and be humble.

Study to show thyself approved unto God, a workman that needeth not to be ashamed, rightly dividing the word of truth.

2 Timothy 2: 15

The Essence of the Bible

Many people have tried to disprove the Bible only to fail and be converted to Christianity – such as Simon Greenleaf, a law professor in the 19th century who doubted the resurrection of God's Son Jesus Christ, but after thorough study concluded its validity.

Josh McDowell tried to prove Christianity was a sham, but after being reproved by friends and further study of the scriptures, said the Bible is trustworthy and historically reliable.

Gary Parker, who held a doctorate in Biology and preached evolution, finally proclaimed God was creator of heaven and earth (information courtesy of David Cloud of *Way of Life* literature).

While the Bible has been constantly re-issued and re-interpreted allowable by 2 Timothy 3: 16: for all scripture is given by instruction of God, and is profitable for doctrine, for reproof, for correction, for instruction in righteousness -- its power to convict the human mind of sin is undisputable.

Consider searching the scriptures for a better way to live – but also learn about Jesus, who said, "Search the scriptures; for in them ye think ye have eternal life; and they are they which testify of me" (John 5: 39).

Wherefore, the people did strive with Moses, and said, Give us water that we may drink . . .   *Exodus 17: 2*

God's Leading

The people were angry because they were hungry and thirsty -- and their leader Moses was not providing provisions to sustain them.

A leader is usually the first one to be criticized when something goes wrong.

Worse, the people made up lies about Moses, accusing him of trying to kill them.

Moses felt the pressure from the people and went to God in prayer to get some answers.

God heard the prayer of Moses and led him to a rock, where Moses struck it with a stick, and out came water.

Know that God is faithful to complete a task that he has ordained.

But criticizing leaders is often vain. Leaders are humans that make mistakes.

Our leader is God Almighty, and Jesus is the one who has entered the heavens to be our priest forever.

For the love of money is the root of all evil, which, while some coveted after, they have erred from the faith . . .
1 Timothy 6: 10

Love of Money Brings Problems

Several people in the Bible let the love of money and material goods get in the way of serving God and having peace.

Jacob deceived his father to get his brother's birthright inheritance and then fearfully left home to escape the jealousy of Brother Esau.

Joseph's brothers sold him into slavery for money -- only to suffer for lack of food years later during a famine and be brought back to Joseph -- to face their sin.

And then there is Christ's disciple Judas, who sold information about Jesus for thirty pieces of silver and hung himself.

Consider the desire for money and whether it is morally right, for the proverb says, In the house of the righteous is much treasure, but in the revenues of the wicked is trouble (Prov. 15: 6).

True riches are with Christ Jesus who rose into heaven and intercedes on behalf of believers to take away sin and give spiritual wealth (Ephesians 1: 7-14).

And he showed me a pure river of water of life, clear as crystal, proceeding out of the throne of God and of the Lamb.

Rev. 22: 1

God's Water of Life

I was walking along a marsh bank at Calabash N.C. when I saw ripples of water constantly hitting the shoreline..

The ripples appeared to be from mud minnows feeding on marsh residue, but upon closer observation, wind driven waves of water rocked floating straw on the surface of the water making small waves like a drummer boy tapping on cymbals.

I walked on and thought about Revelation Chapter 22 – where the water of life flows freely from the throne of God with a tree of life on each side of the river.

The Bible says, My doctrine shall drop as the rain; my speech shall distill as the dew, as the small rain upon the tender herb, and as the showers upon the grass (Deut. 32: 2).

Consider the beauty in nature but also the spirit of God, which allows us to see it.

If our minds are cluttered with worries, doubts, or fear, we are unable to see beauty in the world, but if we know Jesus, our minds are clear to enjoy the works of God in nature.

A word fitly spoken is like apples of gold in pictures of silver.   *Proverbs 25: 11*

Words

My mother rarely spoke. Possibly, it was because of her Indian descent and upbringing.

But mainly it was because of her quiet faith in God.

She claimed the Bible's wisdom was her guide for life, such as the scripture in Eccl. 5: 2 which says, Be not rash with thy mouth, and let not thine heart be hasty to utter any thing before God; for God is in heaven, and thou upon earth; therefore let thy words be few (Eccl 5: 2).

She let her work and great faith speak. She worked full time, taught Sunday school, and raised two boys.

I admired her quiet faith and ability to refrain from talking about people or getting upset with life's problems.

"The Lord will take care of it," she'd say when something bad happened.

God's Son Jesus also cautions us to speak, "For by thy words thou shalt be justified, and by thy words, thou shalt be condemned" (Matthew 12: 37).

In contrast, the Bible says, Pleasant words are like a honeycomb, sweet to the soul, and health to the bones (Prov. 16: 24).

Wherefore laying aside all malice, and all guile, and hypocrisies, and envies, and all evil speaking, As newborn babes, desire the pure milk of the word, that ye may grow by it, If so be ye have tasted that the Lord is gracious.
1 Peter 2: 1-3

Which Bible?

When I heard visiting pastors from a nearby Christian law school preach the meaning of Biblical words from original languages, I was encouraged to perform personal Bible study.

But from which Bible?

There are numerous Bibles available for studying, along with interlinear English transliterations from the Greek and Hebrew languages that give insight to God's word.

I eventually bought a New Schofield Reference Bible, because I like the introductions to each biblical book, the sub-headings to each story, the subject chain references, and clarifications from the old English text (such as the word "nigh" being translated to "near").

There is a word pronunciation guide, footnotes to major subjects, summaries of doctrines and dispensations, a list of God's covenants, an index to annotations, a concise concordance, and maps!

The original Schofield Reference Bible was published in 1909 with a revision in 1917. The New Schofield Reference Bible was published in 1967 and references new archaeology discoveries.

Consider your work each day but also a journey into God's word in the calm of the morning or evening reading the Bible. You'll be glad to find out the truth about God who created you and your purpose.

God is our refuge and strength, a very present help in trouble.   *Psalms 46: 1*

God's Saving Presence

I was let off on a deserted street corner in a small town on a cold rainy night in Kentucky in the year 1971 about 2:30 one humid morning shortly after I had fought off a threat from a man who had picked me up earlier in St. Louis only to stop at the end of a deserted swamp road.

I was unnerved.

Fortunately, I had gotten a bottled drink at a restaurant stop to use as a weapon minutes before the swamp road exit, for God was preparing me for battle.

I walked through the rain towards an "open" sign and entered a diner. I had a cup of coffee from a smiling waitress, and then I resumed my journey eastward.

I thought, *had I not turned to the Lord for safety earlier, there's no telling what might have happened.*

Jesus wasn't always in control of his situation: he found himself in a desert for forty days and being confronted by the devil.

But Jesus stayed around God's throne and told the devil, "Begone Satan, for it is written, Thou shalt worship the Lord thy God, and him only shalt thou serve", (Matthew 4: 10.

When sensing danger, always look to the Lord for safety, and He will guide you into a safe place.

As newborn babes, desire the pure milk of the word, that ye may grow by it, if so be ye have tasted that the Lord is gracious. 1 Peter 2: 2

The Curious One

The clouds moved offshore and the sun began to dry the ground as people unloaded their boats and made their way to the Intracoastal Waterway to fish or get some cool air over the water.

I parked my car, grabbed a couple of crab pots from the trunk along with a bucket, and tucked them under my arm. With the other hand and arm, I picked up a bag containing ice cream and chicken thighs I had just purchased at the store.

Carrying my load and making my way down the hill to the little pier at the waterway, I met a smiling girl and began to share the beauty of God and the day, while she did likewise.

She didn't look any more than thirty years old, with clear skin, a petite form, and a teenage graduation ring set with a garnet stone on her finger.

Our smiles and joy for life and God captivated each other and we talked about God, fishing, and life. We eventually embraced as if we'd known each other all our lives, which solidified our kindred spirits and love for humanity.

She continued to talk, "I don't know what I'm going to do. They've run me out of the church, crime is so bad, and my husband takes drugs and has confessed to molesting girls."

Her eyes sparkled with understanding against the backdrop of her black hair.

"Don't know where I'm supposed to be and need a home."

"But our home is not on earth: it's in heaven," I responded.

After more dialogue, we made our way back to my car to get a little blue book I had written years ago because I knew she'd find the answer to her problem.

And then her inquisitive young travelling accomplice arrived wondering what we were talking about.

"God," I responded.

Slim, 16, with long blond hair swaying in the wind, bare feet, and cut off shorts, she wanted to know more about God. Interest covered her face like a cat's stare.

And so we talked, and she found understanding.

Experiencing God's love for others draws people to see what the joy is about.

It was not in vain when Jesus said, "This is my commandment, that ye love one another, as I have loved you.

O Lord God of my salvation, I have cried day and night before thee. *Psalms 88: 1*

The Faithful Psalmist

Psalms 88 depicts a man who knows the Lord's salvation but is in constant misery, as if he is in a dungeon somewhere.

But what person who knows the Lord isn't afflicted in some way?

Salvation from sin does not always guarantee the knowing presence of God!

For the psalmist says in Verse 14, "Why hidest thou face from me?"

We just have to know God is here, in any circumstance.

We have to feel him in our hearts, minds, soul, and faith. "O how I love thee O God."

One of my favorite scriptures is Ephesians 4:30: And grieve not the Holy Spirit of God, by whom ye are sealed unto the day of redemption.

Sealed. And the Apostle Paul says nothing can separate us from the love of God (Romans 8:35).

Life is certainly not fair, but humility brings God to life, and Psalms 88 glorifies God in salvation and in trouble.

Again, the kingdom of heaven is like a merchant man, seeking fine pearls, Who, when he had found one pearl of great price, went and sold all that he had, and bought it.
Matt. 11: 45-46

Finding the Kingdom

Finding the Kingdom of Heaven is also like getting on an unfamiliar boat and going on a cruise to destination unknown.

You can't see the destination because of the weather, waves, or distance.

And it takes awhile to get comfortable, because the boat is rocking and you're sitting on a hard bench that occasionally jolts.

But once you get used to it, there's the pleasure of floating on water.

It's the same way reading the Bible and learning about God.

Opening the first page of scriptures can be the most difficult -- like lifting a foot off the dock and getting into the boat the first time

"How can I trust God?" you might ask. Or "What about my sin!"

All that is explained in the Book of Romans, which stipulates the central truths of Christianity.

There is therefore, now no condemnation to them who are in Christ Jesus, who walk not after the flesh, but after the Spirit (Romans 8:1).

Christ hath redeemed us from the curse of the law, being made a curse for us; for it is written, Cursed is everyone that hangeth on a tree.   Gal. 3: 13

God's Providential Curse

One wouldn't normally think of God making a curse but that is what he did in the beginning of life when he cursed a serpent for deceiving Eve. He also cursed the ground because of Adam's disobedience (Genesis 3: 17).

Curse means to abhor, detest, or cast evil upon, according to the dictionary.

God says he will curse anyone who disobeys his law. The maladies of being cursed are in Deuteronomy 27: 15-26 and 28: 15-68.

The good news is the blessing in Deuteronomy 28: 1-14, if we obey God's law.

God in his infinite wisdom knew man couldn't obey all the laws, so he sent Jesus to be a curse for us (Galatians 3:13). With him being crucified on the cross, he took our sins to the grave.

Jesus noted the curse in St. Matthew 25: 41, in a parable of his return to earth and God ordering the cursed to depart.

Jesus Christ has defeated the curse (Gal. 3: 14).

And there shall be no more curse, but the throne of God and of the Lamb shall be in it [the river of life], and his servants shall serve him (Rev. 22: 3).

I will speak, that I may be refreshed; I will open my lips and answer.   *Job 32: 20*

The Refreshing Word

God's word refreshes the soul, relieves the mental burden to share good news, and contributes to learning more about a God who created us.

Elihu witnessed God, "The Spirit of God hath made me, and the breath of the Almighty hath given me life"; he said in Job 33: 4.

But refraining to speak God's words may cause grief and sadness.

This is the problem Elihu faced after hearing friends trying to console Job's suffering condition and having no good answer. Elihu said his belly was about to burst!

That's what holding in the word of God does.

In some ways, we are inviting someone's grief and pain because we are silent to invoke God's word of encouragement!

But Elihu was also wise enough to know that his words might be in vain, and he talked of God's discernment: "Teach us what we shall say unto him; for we cannot order our speech by reason of darkness" (Job 37: 19).

No, we can't. We need God's presence, and through Jesus Christ we can speak words that are right for other people and healthy for our lives.

This is the law of the beasts, and of the fowl, and of every living creature that moveth in the waters, and of every creature that creepeth upon the earth.   Lev. 11: 46

The Vulture Place

The moon was visible over a forest of tall pine trees at sunset when I saw vultures flying in circles looking for prey.

I sat in my car eating a sandwich and thinking about Leviticus 11, where God forbids man to eat vultures

Yet vultures have their place in the world to clean up dead carcasses.

Surely it was a sad thing for vultures to be around the dead saints at the destruction of Jerusalem in Psalms 79: 2.

There are also vultures in Deuteronomy 28: 26 -- where if a person has disobeyed God's commandments, he or she may become a victim of vultures and no man will be able to shoo them away!

But consider Jesus, whose body was entombed and saved from vultures.

He arose into heaven and appeared to men to open their understanding about how to be saved from sin.

He continues to give understanding about repentance and remission of sins today throughout the world (Luke 24: 47).

Wherefore, putting away lying, speak every man truth with his neighbor; for we are members one of another.`
Ephesians 4: 25

The Vanity of Lying

I was driving my car one rainy night and saw a woman walking along the side of the road.

I pulled the car to the side and stopped. In a short amount of time, she arrived at the front door and opened it.

We looked each other over while the rain was dripping off her upturned black coat collar, and I invited her in.

She said her car had broken down.

But there was no car.

Then she said she was hungry and needed to go to the store to buy groceries. She said she had money, but when we got to the store, she claimed to have none.

She continued to lie while I listened in amazement.

The Bible says the Lord hates lying in Proverbs 6: 16-17 and 12: 22.

And it is with good reason, because he can't bless a person who fails to tell the truth.

I gave her a few dollars for food, and then we had prayer.

Know Jesus can take away lying lips and give a new life of righteousness by faith.

And God said, Let the waters bring forth abundantly the moving creature that hath life . . .   *Genesis 1:20*

God's Sea and Bird Life

God created life in the sea but there sure wasn't much this day as my friend James and I stared at the water below the pier wondering if they were any fish in the ocean at all.

Then a pelican all of three feet tall walked up behind us, jumped up on the guard rail, and stared at us.

Time seemed to stop for a few seconds.

James smugly looked over and said, "Make a good picture."

"Maybe for a booklet," I concurred.

And so I grabbed my camera knowing the bird would fly away before I could get a picture, but he continued to stare at us as if he had posed for pictures before.

I kept the right side of the camera view spared for a book title in the sky and took a picture with the pelican on the left,

And I showed James. He said, "Now that's nice."

And that's how the third printing cover for *Quiet Heavens* developed!

Consider the fowls of heavens that God made on the fifth day of creation but also consider Jesus, who takes away the sin of the world.

There cometh a woman of Samaria to draw water. Jesus saith unto her, "Give me to drink."   John 4: 7

The Long Talk

The longest recorded conversation between a man and a woman in the New Testament is in John 4 where Jesus is tired from a journey, sits down by a well of water, and begins to talk with a woman addressing her seven times.

This woman found out more about Jesus in one time period than any other person on earth.

That's what we should do! Get to know Jesus!

"Sir, give me this everlasting water that I thirst not, neither come here to draw" (John 4:15), she said after he had explained to her that he was the living water.

Consider this dialogue but also the unspoken words between the two: there was no talk about sports, jokes, or the weather.

It was a needful talk – a burden from God to share good news and yet be refreshed physically.

Everyone has some type of burden.

Wouldn't it be nice to get encouragement from each other in the spirit of God?

And Joseph saw his brethren, and he knew them, but made himself strange unto them, and spoke roughly unto them . . .   *Genesis 42: 7*

The Rough Answer

Joseph answered his brothers roughly because he despised them for abandoning him years earlier.

Then he found himself crying and overcome with emotions because he was withholding food from them in a time of famine and disguising himself as another person.

Eventually, he would reveal himself, but because of his pride lots of people suffered. His brothers were jailed; their father was worried about the missing sons; and younger brother Benjamin had to make a needless trip.

Obviously, this was Joseph's way of having vengeance on his brothers.

The proverb is true: the poor useth entreaties, but the rich answereth roughly (Prov. 18: 23).

Consider a response to someone who may have offended you in the past. A firm answer of righteousness may be called for, or possibly words of compassion.

But look to God for all things, along with presenting Jesus as a loving Savior who died for our sins.

As he came forth of his mother's womb, naked shall he return to go as he came, and shall take nothing of his labor, which he may carry away in his hand.   Eccl. 5: 15

Temporal Goods

Solomon, the supposed author of the Book of Ecclesiastes, gave us wisdom about accumulating too much material goods because upon death they will be left behind.

Every week there's an auction in town that has many goods – both new and old.

In most cases, someone has died and their goods are being sold off.

It's a reminder that life on earth is temporary and that someone else will get the goods!

Solomon had more to say: Therefore I hated all my labor which I had taken under the sun, because I should leave it unto the man that shall be after me; Eccl. 2: 18.

The psalmist of Psalms 49: 10 expressed a similar view: For he [God] seeth that wise men die; likewise, the fool and the stupid person perish, and leave their wealth to others.

In contrast, A good man leaveth an inheritance to his children's children . . . (Prov. 13: 22).

But consider wisdom from Jesus, who told us not to lay up for ourselves treasure on earth, but in heaven . . . for where your treasure is, there will be your heart also (Matt. 6:19-21).

Jesus said, "I am the resurrection and the life he that believeth in me, though he were e dead, yet shall he live.
John 11: 25

Hope for Old Age

I was delivering mail one day and walked upon the front porch to put the mail in the box but noticed the screen door was open.

Mr. Thurston was sitting in a wooden chair on a spotless oak floor that had been thoroughly cleared of rugs and furniture.

"You okay Mr. Thurston?" I asked as I began fingering the mail for the next delivery.

"Hurting bad," he muttered.

"Anything you can do about it?" I asked.

"Yeah, die," he responded.

But that's the feeling a person gets when old and feeling pain: the good years are gone and now there's sadness and hurt.

The Bible says, The days of our years are threescore years and ten; and if, by reason of strength, they be fourscore years, yet is their strength labor and sorrow . . . (Psalms 90: 10).

But consider Jesus, who gives us hope to look forward to life after death. This attitude keeps us living in the Spirit of life and have joy to the end.

For God hath not given us the spirit of fear, but of power, and of love, and of a sound mind.   *1 Tim. 1: 7*

Power in the Lord

The scriptures keep us in the right mind.

They give us encouragement to stand up against the wiles of the devil and not let him shut us up. We can rise and take a stand for what's right and not submit to ungodly rules and mandates that rip our God-given freedoms and liberty away.

Consider being the kind of Christian that fights for Christ and not the kind that backs down and allows the enemy to take over.

Stand up for life! Stand up for freedom! Stand up for liberty! Stand up for Jesus! And don't deny him.

We have been warned: "But whosoever shall deny me before men, him will I also deny before my Father, who is in heaven" (Matt. 10: 33).

Now is the time with all the anti-godly statements being issued to counter them with Biblical scriptures and the power of God's word.

Know Jesus and know power, for he has victory over sin, death, and ungodliness.

Jeanette Cole

And he said unto them, "Take heed, and beware of covetousness, for a man's life consisteth not in the abundance of the things which he possesseth. Luke 12: 15

The Hoarder

Covetousness is an ungodly desire to accumulate goods that serve a selfish purpose which violates God's tenth commandment.

I went to a friend's house one day and she told me she wanted a fence built around her yard. She walked around and showed me where she wanted it.

But there was junk everywhere on the perimeter!

There were lots of trees, poles, and limbs, which were being used as a makeshift fence.

"There's no room for a fence," I told her. "A person can't even walk in the area."

She didn't want to hear it -- and started walking in the direction she wanted a fence with her head bowed.

After a few minutes, she stopped and looked at me and said, "Pray for me, please."

She reached out her cold nervous hand to meet mine for prayer.

I thought of Jesus and the parable about the man who hoarded goods only to be confronted by God about losing his soul (Luke 12: 16-21).

Too many goods and materials are a distraction from serving God. The Bible says, But my God shall supply all your need according to his riches in glory by Christ Jesus (Philippians 4: 19).

And he came unto his father, and said, "My father: and he said, Here am I; who art thou, my son?"   Gen. 27: 18

Jacob's Judgment

Isaac had a feeling that the man reaching out to him was not his firstborn son Esau, so he questioned him.

It was deceitful brother Jacob who dressed himself up as Esau.

After Jacob stole his brother Esau's blessing by deceiving their father, he ran away -- until he had to face God and Esau years later.

There wouldn't be any deceit now because an angel would knock Jacob's leg out of joint in Genesis 32.

But that's what sin does: it brings fear, worry, and judgment – to be met by God's presence, if he chooses.

But consider Jesus, who died for our sins and allows us to meet God face to face without punishment when we confess our sin and come into agreement with his virgin birth and death on the cross to take away sin.

"Come unto me all ye that labor and are heavy laden; and I will give you rest. Take my yoke upon you, and learn of me . . . ." (Matt. 11: 28-29).

And I say also unto thee, That thou art Peter, and upon this rock I will build my church, and the gates of Hades shall not prevail against it.   Matt. 16: 18

The Open Church

It was snowing outside with a foot of it already on the ground as I exited a motel room from where I had spent the night on a weekend pass from the Army, and I was petrified.

At 17 years old, with the Vietnam war continuing, I was certain to be deployed.

I looked across the street at snow filled yards to see a church with red brick exterior and white doors that beckoned me in.

I crossed the street and entered the doors. I sat down and wondered about life. I had joined the Army because I had nowhere else to go. Forced bussing had sent me across town to an unhealthy situation. I had no job. And I had little monetary support.

A clock ticked aloud in the background as the congregation became quiet and the preacher arrived..

The Bible says of King David, that I may dwell in the house of the Lord all the days of my life, to behold the beauty of the Lord, and to inquire in his temple (Psalms 27" 4).

That's what I did that day, I inquired, – and to make sure my faith was sure.

Consider your faith -- and the church -- that despite its imperfections, the doors are usually open when doubtful, scared, or sinful.

But know also God's Son Jesus, who's faith in God built the church and offers salvation to anyone who inquires and receives him as Savior.

Know also not to forsake the assembly of believers, as the manner of some is, but exhort one another. Heb. 10: 25

The Temple Consecration

When the temple was destroyed in A.D. 70, it was no coincidence Jesus became a temple for people to worship.

Jesus had said, "Destroy this temple and in three days I will raise it up"; John 2: 19.

And in three days after his death, he was raised up into heaven.

Consider ungodly attempts to shut down or destroy worldly temples but also consider Jesus, the true temple for a congregation of believers who are written in the Book of Life (verse 27).

It's a spiritual thing one might say.

Well, certainly. The spirit is life -- the physical body and earthly structures are temporal.

Not by accident, the word "temple" is derived from the Latin "tempus"– surfaces along the forehead.

And we know Jesus was talking about his body.

Consider worshipping God in a church or temple but also at the throne of God that never closes; the gates of it shall not be shut at all by day; for there shall be no might there (Rev. 21: 25).

The Book of Revelation says, And I saw no temple in it [about the throne of God]; for the Lord God Almighty and the Lamb are the temple of it (Rev. 21: 22).

"Ought not Christ to have suffered these things, and to enter into his glory?" Luke 24: 26

The Suffering Christ

Persecuted, scourged, and ridiculed by authorities, the suffering Christ kept his focus on serving God with joy (see Hebrews 12: 2).

Consider the humiliation this man must have felt, being defamed in court, mocked, and disrespected, though he had God's wisdom and had taught people in the temple.

Come up with a good idea that has God's blessing, and the world culture wants to deny it.

Most of us have been there, but it's how we find our place to achieve great things with the confidence of God and Jesus Christ independently of Satan's ways.

God had ordained the birth and work of Jesus from the beginning by the prophet Isaiah (see Chapter 11, 42, 49-57) -- to glorify God, which has helped many people find peace in an otherwise troubled world.

Consider your suffering. But also know Jesus has died for it and rose to sit on God's right hand to give peace.

Let this mind be in you, which was also in Christ Jesus . . . But made himself of no reputation, and took upon him the form of a servant, and was made in the likeness of men.

Philippians 2: 5-7

The Small Jesus

Consider Jesus, though small in stature and rejected, became a redeemer of sin for everyone on earth. His faith was great, and his power was from knowing God.

The ruler Pilate had told Jesus that he had the power to either release him from captivity or have him crucified.

But the power was in Jesus' favor, and he let Pilate know it.

Jesus said, "Thou couldest have no power at all against me, except it were given thee from above . . ." (John 19: 11).

Jesus was familiar with the court process. He had attended a preliminary hearing before Annas -- and an informal trial before Caiaphas and the Sanhedrin.

As a humble man, Jesus withstood each of them to follow the will of his Father in Heaven.

There is a proverb of a poor man who delivered a city in Ecclesiastes 9: 15 after a great king besieged it, but the poor man's wisdom was despised.

Such was the case of Jesus, who was about to deliver the people from the bondage of sin and fear of death.

Cast thy burden upon the Lord, and he shall sustain thee; he shall never suffer the righteous to be moved
Psalms 55: 22

The Burdens of Life

David is talking about the burden of King Saul trying to kill him.

Hundreds of years earlier, the Israelites had a burden of physical labor working for the Egyptians. They had to gather rock, straw, and cement to make brick for buildings.

Nevertheless, God heard the burdensome prayers of the people and provided mercy.

For us, there may be a burden from environmental pollution, flooding, forest fires, or electro-magnetic hazards, but God is still available to listen to our prayers and have mercy.

Maybe there is a relationship burden, in which case we are to pray for each other. We boldly come to the throne of God and ask for guidance.

But if we have a burden of sin, Jesus is here to help us. "For my yoke is easy, and my burden is light," he said (Matt. 6: 30).

Hopefully, we have the burden to witness God, as faithful believers in the past have done.

Now, therefore, hearken unto me, O ye children; for blessed are they who keep my ways.   *Prov. 8: 32*

Wisdom Gives Life

God's way was not considered one sunny day in Midwestern Kansas in 1975 when my friend Jamie decided to go for a swim and dive off a 25 foot embankment high above a placid lake amidst tall trees and rock outcroppings.

I was sitting off a good distance on a dirt path and nursing a sports injury from the previous day.

Well, Jamie took off on a running head start and splashed head first in the water – only he never came back up.

Some blood did though, and my close friend Gregory promptly dove into the water to retrieve Jamie and bring him to the surface, bloody mess and all.

I waved down a passing motorboat operator, who came and put Jamie in the boat and took him to the nearest boat ramp for a trip to the hospital.

Consider Biblical instruction in times of uncertain plunges in life: Hear my son, and receive my sayings, and the years of thy life may be many (Prov. 4: 10).

And now we have Jesus, the Son of God who came to save us from sins and give us a new beginning.

The Lord is righteous in all his ways and holy in all his works.   *Psalms 145: 17*

The Righteous God

In the 1990's government agencies were required to construct wider sidewalks and entrances to bathrooms for wheelchairs and handicapped people.

One of those bathrooms was on a steep hill in a National Park where I used to work in maintenance.

My boss made our crew install rebar six inches apart throughout a circular walk 100' long and 4' wide!

An armored tank could have driven over that walk after the concrete was poured. He definitely wanted it right.

Consider the righteousness of God.

His work is perfect; for all his ways are justice, a God of truth and without iniquity, just and right is he (Deut. 32: 4).

Following God's way are perfect, and though we can't always live up to it, God is certainly pleased with our effort.

Know also God's Son Jesus, who took our errors to the cross. Without a burden of sin, we can perform good works.

The statutes of the Lord are right, rejoicing the heart; the commandment of the Lord is pure, enlightening the eyes (Psalms 19: 8).

As the Lord commanded Moses, so he numbered them in the wilderness o Sinai. *Numbers 1: 19*

Numbers

Numbers, the title of the third book of the Bible derives its name from the Greek word *Arithmoi* and refers to the two numberings of the Israelites in the wilderness in Chapters 1 and 26.

But a better title would have been *Bemidbar*, the Hebrew title, which means "wanderings"; the book of Numbers shows the wanderings of the people in the wilderness for forty years.

But consider God and numbers. He made fun of numbers when he told Abraham to count an unlimited number stars in heaven in Genesis 15: 5.

God's prophet Daniel came up with several sets of numbers in the Book of Daniel, referring to beasts, horns, weeks, and years while predicting the future.

Jesus used numbers on a few occasions, the most prominent about forgiving someone in Matt. 18: seventy times seven times.

But the most important number is *one*: Hear O Israel: the Lord our God is one Lord (Deut. 6: 4).

The way to find the Lord is through the one Savior Jesus Christ by confession and forgiveness of sin.

Go ye into all the world, and preach the gospel to every creature.

Mark 16: 15

The Pilgrim Tract Society

The Pilgrim Tract Society mails gospel tracts to such places as East Africa, Brazil, Malawi, Nigeria, Ghana, England, and Haiti, to name a few.

Chris Hancock, Director of PTS, said in an Autumn 2020 newsletter, "Gospel tracts, Bibles, and Christian literature are now being distributed all over Nigeria. We pray that a great harvest of souls for Jesus will occur from the Word of God being sown in Nigeria from this container. The 40-foot container that we shipped to Nigeria arrived and was unloaded on October 12."

For a small donation sent to the PTS, anyone can receive up to 1200 different gospel tracts – written by faithful people of the past from all over the world who testify of the power of God and Jesus Christ.

How wonderful it is to know that people who are being oppressed or enslaved in other countries can now learn about the saving power of Jesus Christ and God Almighty.

Consider the literature messages but also the ministry. Each of us has some kind of talent, and we should use it to share God's word.

And Eliab, his eldest brother, heard when he spoke unto the men; and Eliab's anger was kindled against David, and he said, "Why camest thou down here? And with whom hast thou left those few sheep in the wilderness? I know thy pride, and the naughtiness of thine heart . . .   *1 Sam. 17: 28*

Pride's Disposition

David heard about a reward for killing a giant named Goliath of the Philistine army; so he went to King Saul for permission to fight.

King Saul said, "Thou are not able to go against this Philistine to fight with him; for thou art but a youth, and he a man of war from his youth."

David wasn't backing down from his request.

"Thy servant slew both the lion and the bear (while guarding the family's sheep). And this uncircumcised Philistine shall be as one of them."

Being given permission to fight Goliath, David slew Goliath and became famous among the people.

But prideful actions usually lead to a downfall, which is what happened to David when King Saul become jealous of him and chased him around the country.

One might wonder what would have happened to David if he humbled himself in front of his brother Elihu and went back home to his father to be a shepherd boy.

But then, David wrote many psalms that glorified God.

Thou shalt not steal.

Ex. 20: 15

The Thief

I heard he was a thief and now I saw it.

He was handling some goods my friend had just bought but had to leave momentarily to move his car closer to the loading area.

"They're someone else's," I said to the intruder.

It fazed him not, and he continued to handle the tools the other man had purchased.

The intruder then looked to a friend for encouragement.

That's what a sinner does – wants to include another person in the crime. Then he can shift the blame, "He did it! I didn't!"

Thieves have a chance to redeem themselves by confession of sin and repentance, but consider the two thieves on the crosses of death beside Jesus.

Jesus forgave one (Luke 23: 43).

But there was no mention of what happened to the other one.

It's best not to steal.

That ye be not slothful, but followers of them who through faith and patience inherit the promises. Heb. 6: 12

Promises

God has made many promises in the Bible but there is one he breached.

It was because the people started complaining about not getting to a land of milk and honey fast enough in Numbers 14: 34.

God certainly won't fulfill a promise for people who complain and disobey orders.

Promises also take place between people, but God is usually left out of the agreement, and then all kinds of problems ensue.

This is why people in Biblical times used to invoke God's name when they were coming to agreement over some matter. They knew God would guarantee the promise.

The most *prominent* promise in scripture is the one given to King David in 2 Samuel 7: 12, where God tells David that one of David's seed will establish a kingdom, which became the form of Jesus Christ.

Now we have God and Jesus Christ.

And this is the promise that he hath promised us, even eternal life (1 John 2: 25).

The sea is his, and he made it, and his hands formed the dry land. Oh, come, let us worship and bow down; let us kneel before the Lord our maker.   *Psalms 95: 5-6*

Lord of the World

Sargassum weed often comes to the shoreline after a storm.

On a recent fishing trip, the floating weed was tangled up on my fishing line.

When I slipped each strand off, there was a myriad of eggs and small mollusks attached to them.

Seaweed is troublesome to fishermen but it is food, shelter, and transportation to much of sea life.

And where did the weed come from?

I thought about how God's flows from the throne of God out of darkness and into light. For anyone who reads it, they are sure to be filled with knowledge and content – such as the life on sea weed.

God brings life from the sea and from his word.

Whosoever is born of God doth not commit sin; for his seed remaineth in him, and he cannot sin, because he is born of God.   1 John 3: 9

The Seed of Life

The Pearl Golf Course borders the Calabash River in North Carolina and is home to a variety of plants.

I hit a golf ball just off the fairway one sunny day into a shallow ditch -- where I found it sitting near some rocks at the bottom.

But before I picked it up, I smelled a pungent sweet odor: there was a patch of peppermint right there on the bank of the gulley.

I don't know how it got there. Maybe some colonial settlers brought it on a boat. Maybe a bird dropped a sprig of it. Or maybe the wind blew a seed there.

But God has made the herb of the field for us and there's nothing better than peppermint to stimulate the digestive system.

Jesus talked about seeds being sown in the ground: "He that soweth the good seed is the Son of man . . . the good seed are the children of the kingdom" . . . (Matt. 13: 37-38).

May we sow the good seed of the Word from the Bible to give people divine guidance and life everlasting.

And the earth was without form, and void; and darkness was upon the face of the deep. And the Spirit of God moved upon the face of the waters.   Gen. 1: 2

Ocean Garden

Being near the ocean's edge is a good place to worship the Lord because it is there God moved upon the face of the waters and formed dry land.

But underneath the ocean is another world; there are miles of darkness and life that man has not discovered.

And who knows what my be floating on top of the water? An alligator was found one day coming from the surf.

But become familiar with the ocean and its ways removes a lot of fear.

It is the same way with God.

Learn a little bit about him from the Bible or another person finds there is a peace unparalleled.

I always say a prayer before I enter the ocean for safety and enjoyment. Fortunately, other than a jelly fish sting or stepping on a wayward shell, I've always come back to the beach okay and refreshed.

There's not much more enjoyment than being in salt water and feeling the lapping waves on a clear day.

Give, and it shall be given unto you . . . .
Luke 6: 38

Sharing and Caring

The day was bright and sunny with a strong wind from the southeast that pushed water and fish near shore.

A middle-aged man from Clarendon North Carolina, Henry, was catching many fish.

"I don't keep many for myself," he said. "I give most to the church, and usually, if I don't have any fish to eat later, they give me some. Everyone shares."

The Bible says the liberal shall be made fat, and he that watereth shall be watered himself (Prov. 11: 25).

We have freely received God's salvation; so we should freely give time and effort to help other people.

Henry sets a wonderful example.

Now these are the commandments, the statutes, and the ordinances . . . . that ye might do them in the land to which ye go to possess it.   Deuteronomy 6: 1

A Guide for Success

God knows what is best for us, and Deuteronomy Chapters 6-8 tells us how to obtain it.

The chapters show how God led his people out of slavery and to a land full of milk and honey. God provided green pastures, cisterns full of water, and camps to live in.

But people who were doubtful about God's words -- and disobedient to his law -- never made it to the good land; the weak in faith succumbed to trials and troubles.

Faithful is what we should be – faithful to the one who established rules for our benefit.

Ho, every one that thirsteth, come to the waters, and he that hath no money; come, buy and eat; yea, come, buy wine and milk without money and without price.
Isaiah 55: 1

The Invitation

How wonderful it is to know we can come to God's throne freely!

It doesn't cost anything, and it doesn't require physical or mental effort!

But it can be difficult to separate oneself from family, friends, and possessions to find the living God.

The devil does not want us to find this peace from God.

He would rather us be in bondage. He wants us to find worldly solutions to problems rather than divine help. And he would do anything to stop the joy that God gives us.

Fortunately, God's son Jesus has defeated the devil. After confession and repentance of personal sin, God will extend blessings of mercy.

Jesus also gives us an invitation in Revelation 3: 20: If any man hears my voice and opens the door, I will come in to him, and will sup with him, and he with me.

Jesus is the living sacrifice for our sins that allows us to find God in the spirit.

A wise man will hear, and will increase learning; and a man of understanding shall attain unto wise counsels, to understand a proverb and the interpretation, the words of the wise and their dark sayings.   *Proverbs 1: 5-6*

Counsel Time

God is a great counselor and there's no better place to receive counseling than in the Book of Proverbs.

There are proverbs about how to stay away from evil, how to be prosperous, and how to get along with people.

Consider also Jesus, the Son of God who had great wisdom about the ways of the world and heaven. He was able to teach the people through parables.

Jesus said whosoever does his sayings is like a rock that withstands inclement weather (Luke 6: 46-99).

His parables in the world and their relation to God's kingdom show there are spiritual answers for any problem.

Turn you at my reproof; behold, I will pour out my spirit unto you, I will make known my words unto you.
Proverbs 1: 23

Searching for Wisdom

I went searching for wisdom one weekend far back in the Shenandoah National Forest on a hunting trip.

It was cold and frigid that day in the woods, and I soon found myself sleeping on a log.

When I awoke, I could barely move, because it was so cold. A squirrel, standing on the bottom of the log stared at me.

As I slipped off the log, a man appeared from the lower woods walking with his shotgun cradled in his arm.

I had a question on my mind about life, and he looked like a man of wisdom and confidence.

After an introductory greeting, I asked this old doctor, "Is there a time in life where a person just gets to know everything?"

"No!" he exclaimed. "There's too much going on all over the world!"

I nodded my head in acceptance and just knew I had asked a stupid question.

Soon after that trip, I found Jesus, and that was really all I needed to know.

I don't know what faith the doctor had that day, but it was stronger than mine.

Nature and wisdom also taught me not to fall asleep on a log on a freezing day.

And thou shalt write them upon the doorposts of thine house, and upon thy gates.   *Deut. 11:20*

The Protective Word

This scripture commands us to post God's word around the living area, and in this story, it may have helped.

I was driving my car out in the country one day looking at property for sale when I saw a man in a field across the street looking at his house.

I stopped because I needed some directions, and I asked him if he liked living in the area.

He said, "You don't want to live here. There's too much crime." He nodded to his house across the street. "Thieves broke in there and stole my television set, guns, and coins."

"Well. Can you put an extra lock on the door?" I asked.

"That won't stop them. They broke the window to get in."

"Have you tried posting God's word somewhere?" I said.

"They don't care."

I left feeling sorrowful for the man, but I know that God has a chance of protecting our property when we post his word.

A simple sign, statute, or image that glorifies God goes a long way toward keeping the devil away.

And they arrived at the country of the Gereasenes, which is opposite Galilee.   Luke 8: 26

Healing the Lunatic

Jesus and his disciples went on a mission to spread the word of God, but on one trip, they came across a lunatic who lived in tombs.

The lunatic approached Jesus and said, "What have I do to with thee, Jesus, thou Son of God, most high? I beseech thee, torment me not."

Jesus wanted to help the man but he needed to know something about him, and he asked, "What is thy name?"

The man answered, "Legion" (because many demons were entered into him).

Jesus got rid of the demons by sending them into some pigs which ran down the mountain and into a river.

Jesus can take away any type of lunacy when we come to him in humble adoration and willingness to change.

When wisdom entereth into thine heart, and knowledge is pleasant unto thy soul, Discretion shall preserve thee, understanding shall keep thee.   *Proverbs 2: 10-11*

God Understands

A young lady was putting up stock in a store when I saw her drop a box of goods and utter a slang word.

She noticed I was looking and said, "I'm sorry."

I said, "God understands. It happens to everyone."

She looked at me with surprise and came towards me and asked, "Can I give you a hug?"

Well, I didn't know what the hug would be for, but I nodded yes, because I noticed her young and worried face needed support.

We exchanged a few more words about life and then she said, "I could talk to you all day!"

I said, "Well, I can't stay here all day, But I have something that can."

I went out to my car to grab a self-help book to find peace with God. It was a book I had written years ago, and I came back and opened the devotions to her curious face as she looked over my shoulder.

"Read a few of these. God can help you when nobody else can."

She thanked me and became calm.

When a temptation comes to displease the holy nature of God, consider being calm and quiet. Know God is in control.

The Lord is near unto those of a contrite heart and humble spirit.

Give, and it shall be given unto you . . .
Luke 6: 38

A Gift from the Cross

At a recent auction there was plaque of the crucified Jesus up for bidding. The statue looked so real with red drops of paint dropping down his face.

I saw it first, but a brother managed to buy it with a low bid.

He put the 18" plaque on a table at his flea market booth, and within an hour, a man came by and said he had to have that plaque.

The brother, knowing the significance of the cross and Jesus, didn't want to sell it, so he upped the price. But the man still wanted the plaque.

After the purchase, the buyer led him to a vehicle and gave him three new Bibles as a gift!

That's what giving does – it returns so much back.

Consider the act of letting go of something to please another person.

But also consider Jesus -- who gave up his life to die for our sins and give us a purpose for living.

Abide in me, and I in you. As the branch cannot bear fruit of itself, except it abide in the vine, no more can ye, except ye abide in me.   John 14: 4

The Productive Life

We cannot produce good works without Jesus.

Talking with ourselves will not get the job done. We have to have an intermediary like Jesus Christ and a good God to help us.

I went to fix a drain pipe one day for a lady who lived out in the country. The pipe was clogged up because water had been backing up on a walkway.

I went outside and dug along the pipe's length a good ways until I found leaves and debris clogging the end of the pipe.

But someone had also put a concrete block near the end of the pipe trying to stabilize it.

The lady looked at it and said, "The guy that did that was living a sinful life."

I thought about it and said, "His work shows it. Buried."

If we have a darkened life without Jesus and God, our works will fail, such as what Jesus described in Matthew 7: 26: a house built on unstable ground.

Righteous, corrective, and faithful works are pleasing to God, and they must come by Christ. He died for our sins, gave us fellowship with God, and produced good works.

*Therefore the Lord himself shall give you a sign;
Behold, the virgin shall conceive, and bear a son, and shall
call his name Immanuel.*   Isaiah 7: 14

A Savior for Mankind

A long time ago there was trouble on the earth because people were corrupt, and there was no law to fix things.

People were in such chaos they looked for a spiritual being to help out (Genesis 4: 26).

So the people began to call upon God, and God made laws to restore order.

That helped a little, but some people couldn't obey the law.

Hundreds of years later, God sent His Son Jesus to earth to save people from their sins and give them better lives.

Oh, there are still some rules, but with Jesus, we are forgiven for the ones we just can't seem to obey.

And that's why there is Christmas!

We can have joy and happiness and a merry Christmas as the miracle from heaven in Jesus Christ.

"That thou art Peter, and upon this rock I will build my church, and the gates of Hades shall not prevail against it

Matthew 16: 18

Eternal Praise and Worship

It was quiet and getting dark as the sun was setting and I was waiting for the doors of the church to open.

A man drove up and opened the doors; I entered the sanctuary and found a seat next to man with a harmonica in his hand, who was ready to join in with the three people on stage beginning to sing.

Consider congregational worship and the right to freely assemble. Faithfully, this church never closed during threats or persecution.

The church continues to welcome people to find new lives by confession of faith and belief.

Know also there is a congregation of the dead, when people wander from the way of understanding to find it (Proverbs 21: 16).

But the psalmist said, I will give thee thanks in the great congregation; I will praise thee among many people (Psalms 35: 18).

If I regard iniquity in my heart, the Lord will not hear me. But verily God hath heard me; he hath attended to the voice of my prayer.   Psalms 66: 18-19

Answered Prayer

Staying on good terms with God goes a long way towards receiving help when it's needed.

My friend Belinda, was driving down the highway when her car tire blew out.

There had been multiple accidents on this highway recently from cars that were sitting on the side of the road. Belinda knew that.

She said, "I prayed and prayed and prayed."

Well, God heard her distress call and sent a man to fix the tire in about 45 minutes.

But consider if she had not known God.

Possibly she would have exited the car prematurely and got hit, or maybe she would have gotten unwelcome assistance, or been a victim of foul play.

Prayer fixes things, not only giving a time of peace but direction on what to do.

And prayer establishes righteousness, for God is a righteous God full of compassion.

The way to have effective prayer to God is first by eliminating sin by Jesus Christ. Then, when there's trouble, God will answer with guidance and mercy.

And let us consider one another to provoke unto love and to good works.   *Hebrews 10: 24*

Sharing the Faith

She was sitting on a bench overlooking the ocean when I saw her with a book open.

"Is that a Bible?" I asked.

It's a Bible," she said.

I had just printed a devotional booklet and wanted to share it with another believer.

She took my book and looked it over – and we began to share our faith.

She said she was a detective who investigated suspicious deaths, but the job was stressful and she was thinking of making a change.

We talked for well over an hour.

Consider that believers in God are unified throughout the world and it's a blessing to get together to share the faith.

We don't always know when, how, or where these events will occur, but in doubtful times, God always provides encouragement from someone.

Wherefore, seeing we also are compassed about with so great a cloud of witnesses, let us lay aside every weight and the sin which doth so easily beset us, and let us run with patience the race that is set before us.   Hebrews 12: 1

A Faithful Work

There are a lot of people in the scriptures who have achieved great things, such as Abraham, King David, and Daniel.

But there are also people in today's world who have been just as faithful.

One is Diane Wilson, a shrimp boat operator who for years protested the dumping of chemicals by Formosa Plastics into Matagorda Bay in Texas.

In one action of protest, she chained herself to a water tower. Another time, she sank her boat in front of Formosa's discharge pipe to make a statement.

Consider the faith of this woman, who endured ridicule, shame, and suffering.

But God saw her through the process. An agreement was made to restrict the discharge of chemical pollutants into the bay, and Formosa would have to construct zero chemical discharge outlets.

Everyone's faith is tested at some time, whether for personal or philosophical reasons. While some people refuse to get involved in debates or problems, others find these are good opportunities to witness for God's righteousness and holiness.

And the woman conceived, and bore a son; and when she saw him that he was a beautiful child, she hid him three months. And when she could not longer hide him, she took for him an ark of bulrushes . . . .   *Exodus 2: 2-3*

God's Saving Grace

The baby Moses was hidden in a basket and floated downstream because an Egyptian Pharaoh was going to kill all the newborn Hebrew children.

Fortunately, downstream, an Egyptian woman had mercy on the baby and retrieved the basket. Ironically, she sent the baby Moses back to his Hebrew mother for nursing.

Moses received mercy as a baby, but he certainly gave none when he saw two men fighting and killed a man.

He then left the area, got married, and worked as a herdsman for his father-in-law, Jethro, who was a Godly man.

Consider that life does not always begin with a good start, but with God, things can change for the better. Moses went on to become a prolific writer, judge, and leader of his people.

For a new life, read about how God can eliminate sins of the past through Christ Jesus and provide a new life (Eph. 4: 17-24).

And the Lord said, Shall I hide from Abraham that thing which I do.   *Genesis 18: 17*

God's Intercession

God wanted to do something about the wickedness in a land called Sodom and Gomorrah, and he called on Abraham for assistance.

But Abraham argued with God about the matter, because he had relatives there.

Abraham wanted God to have compassion on the people, so he prayed for mercy.

After prayer, Abraham returned to his place (Genesis 18: 33).

How great is this action of Abraham to put things in God's hands and return to his place!

Often we should return to our place after consulting God with prayer -- to let God work.

I am reminded of Psalms 119: 126 in a time of lawlessness, such as what we are witnessing today in America, which says: It is time for thee, Lord, to work; for they have made void thy law.

The city of Sodom was destroyed but Abraham's nephew and family were saved, except for Lot's wife, who looked back at the carnage.

We often get called to intercede in particular matters such as Abraham, but may we be wise enough to return to our place and let God work out things.

Forever; O Lord, thy word is settled in heaven. Thy faithfulness is unto all generations; thou hast established the earth, and it abideth.   *Psalms 119: 89-90*

God's Word through the Generations

The word of God is generational, and there was no better example of it one day than when I saw an old book that had been published in 1888 lying in the middle of old items for sale at an auction.

I opened the book, *Golden Words for Daily Counsel*, with its weathered and brown edged pages to 365 devotions printed by The Thomas Crowell Company in New York and composed by Anna Harris Smith of Boston, Massachusetts; it was edited by her husband.

Anna Smith, I learned later, had also started an animal rescue mission which continues today.

But consider the work of this book project, to gather sermon material at a time of little technology. Each page would have to be typed, edited, and arranged by a printing company for publication.

But sharing God's word is worth it. It keeps us in the right place and helps other people find God.

For the Lord is good; his mercy is everlasting, and his truth endureth to all generations. (Psalms 100: 5).

And the temple of God was opened in heaven, and there was seen in his temple the ark of his covenant . . .
Revelation 11: 19

The "Ark" of the Covenant

The ark has been described as a coffin, container for the Ten Commandments, a sacrificial offering podium, and even an energy weapon. (After all, the camp of Jericho was taken without a shot being fired.)

But one thing is certain: it is where God met man.

Consider the importance of this box (as it was described by one expository).

It was transported around the country by not only it owners, but enemies, over water, rough terrain, and through war.

It had been adorned with tapestry, and it was even idolized when the Philistines captured it.

Ultimately, the only items found in the ark were the two tablets of stone inscribed with the Ten Commandments (2 Chronicles 5: 10), which is enough to make any man shiver.

There are many references to the ark in the scriptures, but the writer of the Book of Hebrews suggests Jesus has taken the place of the ark.

A minister of the sanctuary, and of the true tabernacle, which the Lord pitched, and not man (Hebrews 8: 2).

Then were the king's scribes called on the thirteenth day of the first month, and there was written according to all that Haman had commanded unto the king . . . Esther 3: 12

The Vain Law

Man has been writing vain law for centuries and none was more appalling than one of the Medes and Persians to exterminate the Jews.

Year later, King Nebuchadnezzar also made a vain law in the Book of Daniel – that demanded all the people come to him when they needed something (Daniel 3: 10).

The word *vain* means emptiness, or something of no value.

Many of man's laws are of no value, which is why they often get repealed.

God had not been consulted.

The wicked love to make vain laws, usually to benefit their own purpose. Never mind that a law may be contrary to God's law.

Fortunately, we have unchanging laws with God as author.

And we have Jesus Christ, who helps free us from the condemnation of the law and allows us to live in the spirit (Romans 8: 2).

Blessed are the meek, for they shall inherit the earth."
Matt. 5: 5

Blessed are the Meek

Being meek is the third message of nine from Jesus' sermon on the mount.

The scripture is a direct quote from Psalms 37: 11: The meek shall inherit the earth, and shall delight themselves in the abundance of peace.

Being meek is of great value to God because he is able to guide a person who is meek: The scripture says, the meek he will guide in judgment (Psalms 25: 9).

The proud person can not be guided by God because there is too much personal thinking going on and stubbornness.

Know that God's Son Jesus was meek and his burden was light -- yet he had great power with God.

We can have this power – by being meek and following God's will.

Consider reading about the meekness of Christ in Matthew 11: 29.

We are also encouraged to put on this meekness in 1 Timothy 6: 11; But thou O man of God, flee these things (speaking of envy, evil, and corruption), and follow after righteousness, godliness, faith, love, patience, and meekness.

> *The wilderness and the solitary place shall be glad for them; and the desert shall rejoice, and blossom like the rose.*
>
> *Isaiah 35: 1*

Blooming Where Planted

Isaiah uses eloquent language about nature when describing kingdom blessings for a re-gathered people..

Another colorful scripture in the book is Isaiah 55: 12, where mountains are singing with joy and trees are clapping their hands experiencing the presence of the Lord.

Possibly these acts of nature only happen in certain places, where God is joyful over a people who begin to worship him.

Cranberries proliferate in the bogs of New England. Ramps, a wild onion with flat green tops only grows in certain places in the mountains, and ginseng is found only at certain elevations on the north side of hills in filtered shade.

The environmental conditions have to be right.

And so does our belief in God.

We might remember when Moses was at a burning bush, God told him it was holy ground.

May we find holy ground to worship God in the place he chooses to enjoy the spirit of God.

And it came to pass, as soon as he came near unto the camp, that he saw the calf, and the dancing; and Moses' anger burned, and he cast the tables out of his hands, and broke them beneath the mount.   Exodus 32: 20

Play and Pray

Moses went to a lot of work climbing a mountain and getting tools ready to etch God's words in stone tablets.

Sadly, it was in vain, because after he descended the mountain and saw the people worshipping a golden calf, he threw down the tablets of stone and they broke.

That only made things worse, because he had to go back up the mountain to make two more tablets.

Everybody suffered in this story: Moses, from his extra work; and the people, who were given a choice to follow the God's will only to rebel and be killed.

But all the people would eventually be plagued because of worship around the golden calf.

I don't know how God eventually ground this golden calf to powder, but I do know that God has power over man and can destroy him at any time because of idolatry.

God allows time for refreshment and exercise in the course of life, but we are certainly not to worship a false god.

There are times to be still and know that God is God, and he wants worship.

As every man hath received the gift, even so minister the same one to another, as good stewards of the manifold grace of God.   1 Peter 4: 10

Made With Love

It was 9: 00 a.m. and I was driving to a lady's house to replace some decking boards when I felt weak and unable to work anywhere -- much less pulling up old boards and nailing new planks down.

So I stopped at a convenience store -- that had a selection of breakfast items and a lady cooking behind the counter.

With a smile on her face, she asked me what I wanted.

"A ham and egg sandwich will be fine," I said.

After eating it in the car, I felt much better. And I went on to complete the job.

Two days later, I stopped at the store again and saw the lady who had made that sandwich, and I thanked her.

She smiled and said, "I made it with love."

What a profound statement from someone I did not know!

I said, "Well, I could tell!"

Consider our daily chores, but also doing them with love.

A little known scripture in Luke 8: 3 tells of several women who gave of their substance before Jesus went and preached to throngs of people about God.

The love for Jesus transcended to other people just as our chores can, when they're made with love.

God is greatly to be feared in the assembly of the saints, and to be had in reverence of all those who are about him.

Psalms 89: 7

Collective Faith

Moses didn't make a plan to free his people from slavery on his own: he met with the elders of Israel beforehand and talked about it in Exodus 4: 29-31.

Meeting in numbers gets things done, when there is an agreement with God.

In this case, everyone had heard about God visiting Moses and the children of Israel, so they believed and made some plans to have total worship in a place he chose.

Without God, our plans are doomed to fail: we are warned in Leviticus 26: 14-26 – that we would be sowing seed in vain.

Certainly Jesus was effective in spreading God's word when he brought together 70 people and sent them out two by two to country towns.

There is no mention of anyone complaining or getting sick; they came back with joy (Luke 10).

For it is written, As I live, saith the Lord, every knee shall bow to me, and every tongue shall confess to God.
Romans 14: 11

Confession

The word confession in the Bible means to agree.

Jesus used the word *confess* in Luke 10: 32 and said if we confess him before men, he will confess us before his Father in heaven (Luke 10: 32).

Confessing Jesus as the Son of God *acknowledges* him as a Savior, who died for our sins and rose into heaven on the third day.

And then there is the popular scripture in the New Testament of Romans 10: 9: if thou confess with thy mouth the Lord Jesus . . . thou shalt be saved.

This is a great statement – to know the kingdom of God is here and separate from a world of sin simply by confession!

But it isn't easy to confess Jesus.

Visiting sins of the past can be a sad and embarrassing time, but after grief and confession, the heavens open and God's forgiveness clears the way for joy.

I will delight myself in thy statutes; I will not forget thy word.   *Psalms 119: 16*

Memorizing Scripture

The psalmist said he would never forget God's word.

In fact, he said it several more times in Psalms 119.

Though horrors by the wicked had taken hold of him, princes had spoken against him, trouble and anguish had consumed him, and he was persecuted by princes, he would not forget God's word.

That's what we need to do: memorize God's word which can save us from a multitude of troubles.

My favorite memory verses are Hebrews 4: 10, where God rests from his work; Ephesians 4: 30, about not grieving God; and the familiar Proverbs 3: 5; trust in the Lord with all thine heart.

Each of those scriptures sustained me through difficult times.

I claimed other scriptures also, such as Deuteronomy 5: 33, when walking with the Lord; and learning to hold words of anger when debating a controversial subject by Prov. 19: 11.

Jesus memorized scriptures and he used them to defeat the devil and give God glory.

But the word of the Lord was unto them precept upon precept, line upon line; here a little, and there a little . . .
Isaiah 28: 13

Create Right

The United States of America has a copyright office in Washington D.C. where works of art, music, and writings are registered.

I'm not sure why it's called "copyright", because the works registered have been *created*. A more likely term for the office might be *create-right*.

But anyway, rights to copy a work are given to an author, or contributors, to copyright. An unauthorized person infringing upon someone's copyright protection could be sued for damages.

But consider the copy rights of scribes to reproduce the Holy Scriptures throughout the centuries.

God gave them this work free of liability to profess his holy word, though many of the copies were not exact reproductions due to language and media changes -- and decomposition changes of original works.

Yet God's word is the same.

Broadman's Commentary stated the scribes were being guided by God with good conscience -- to write Biblical truths for the advancement of spiritual life and discernment for the people.

Consider man's right to copy right, but also God's work to create right and be glorified in the heavens and on earth.

How long wilt thou forget me, O Lord? Forever? How long wilt thou hide thy face from me?   Psalms 13: 1

God Missing?

Sometimes it seems like God is missing when we need him most.

But maybe he just gets quiet, gets tired of our foolishness, or more than likely, waiting for us to get right with him.

Take for instance the man Job who suffered so much and couldn't find God's solace for the longest time. Worse, Job blamed God for his trouble.

But God was in the background the whole time, and he finally came in a whirlwind and confronted Job.

Maybe he wouldn't have come in such a strong wind had Job not been so arrogant.

Jesus went missing one time -- after his friend Lazarus got sick and died. Days later, he showed up at the cave's entrance to bring Lazarus back to life.

But God is never missing. He is always here.

We are to be faithful and call on his name to know he is here.

Vanity of vanities, saith the Preacher, vanity of vanities; all is vanity. *Ecclesiastes 1: 2*

Solomon's Futility

King Solomon talks mostly about life being in vain,
He says work is vain, play is vain, and warns wisdom is vain.

However, Solomon does say a couple of positive things: there is nothing better for a man, than that he should eat and drink, and that he should make his soul enjoy good is his labor (Eccl. 2: 24); Fear God, and keep his commandments, for this is the whole duty of man (Eccl. 12: 13).

It's always amazing to see a speaker of God's word come around to a righteous conclusion after speaking vain words.

But thinking life is vain is not a healthy attitude. Worse, we would suffer judgment from Almighty God for being idle and unbelieving.

With God's Son Jesus, who gives us access to God and a purpose to live – we have joy each day to live in the fullness of God and do good works.

The proverbs of Solomon, the son of David, king of Israel: To know wisdom and instruction; to perceive the words of understanding . . .   *Proverbs 1: 1-3*

The Proverbs Woman

The Book of Proverbs gives us wisdom, and my mother gave a fine example of it one day.

We had travelled to Washington D.C in 1965 to see a Washington Senators-New York Yankees baseball game for my birthday, but she wanted to do some shopping before the game.

We went into a store and she got a hat, but after we had walked a few blocks, she stopped on the sidewalk and said, "Kenny, I've got to go back. I forgot to pay for this hat!"

I looked at her crazily because we had already walked several blocks from the store on that hot day and who would care about the hat. But I was only 12 and had a lot to learn.

She knew failing to pay for that hat would bother her conscience and produce God's judgment: her work would suffer, and she might even be charged for stealing.

So she went back and paid for the hat, while I sat at the base of a monument.

But that was my mother, who was raised in a Baptist Church on the Reservation and who constantly quoted The Book of Proverbs. She was righteous, quiet, humble, and hard working.

Consider advice from the world, but also the scriptures, which give wisdom.

"... Your sheaves stood round about, and made obeisance to my sheaf."   Gen. 37: 7

Fulfilling a Dream

There's no better example of fulfilling a dream than when Joseph dreamed his brothers' bundles of grain would obey his bundles.

And that's what happened years later when Joseph's brothers ran out of food and came to Joseph for help.

Joseph, as you may know, had become a ruler in Egypt and ended up supplying his brothers and father grain in a time of drought.

Joseph also had a dream about the moon and eleven stars obeying him (speaking of his brothers and possibly his father).

Joseph's dream again came true when the brothers found themselves at Joseph's mercy and not being put in jail.

But Joseph certainly had trouble fulfilling these dreams – he was left in a pit to die and later jailed because of a false accusation of adultery.

Consider Joseph's dreams but also Jesus, who fulfilled a vision to die for the people's sins and rise into heaven.

Only God could have pre-determined such an event to happen to save the people from presumptuous sins.

Trust in the Lord with all thine heart; and lean not unto thine own understanding.   *Proverbs 3: 5*

God's Understanding

God's understanding is infinite. He will have compassion and patience over any situation that seems unbearable when we believe it.

A psalmist said the sorrows of death compassed him, and the pains of sheol got hold of him, but he called upon the name of the Lord and found help (Psalms 116).

When you just can't figure out something, it's time to trust God.

Proverbs 3: 3 helps us get God's understanding: Let not mercy and truth forsake thee; bind them about thy neck; write them upon the table of thine heart.

In other words, it's not a mental feeling: it's a whole body experience. You can't reform one without reforming the other, for God knows the thoughts and intents of the soul.

Reformation comes by Jesus Christ and submitting oneself in the fullness of the body to receive redemption for wrong doings and a coming to the knowledge and understanding of God in the Spirit.

May the God of our Lord Jesus Christ, the Father of glory give you the spirit of wisdom and revelation in the knowledge of him . . . the eyes of your understanding being enlightened (Ephesians 1 : 17-18).

But the Spirit of the Lord departed from Saul, and an evil spirit from the Lord troubled him.   *1 Samuel 16: 14*

God's Rule over an Earthly King

God is usually thought of as a good God but he can be harsh, like when he sent an evil spirit on King Saul.

King Saul got in trouble with God when he failed to destroy the goods of the Amalekites in a war. The Amalekites had showed no mercy to the Hebrew children in an earlier war, so God wanted vengeance.

From the day of Saul's disobedience, Saul's kingship was doomed, and the young man David would become king.

David stopped some of God's evil spirit by playing music, but the movement had begun to replace Saul.

Consider the authority of God: he is sovereign to make indiscriminate choices to assign evil or good.

God's power over man is aptly described by Isaiah the prophet: I form the light, and create darkness; I make peace, and create evil; I, the Lord, do all these things (45: 7).

Fortunately, we have Jesus who has broken the curse of God to give us peace (Galatians 3: 13-14).

Oh, give thanks unto the Lord, for he is good; for his mercy endureth forever. Psalms 136: 1

God's Mercy

God gives us mercy even when it is not deserved.

I was on a field training exercise one week in the Army in Kansas and was in charge of providing communications to the tank commanders.

On the second day in the field, I got a call on the radio saying a field phone on a tank was down; so I hurried to the port side port of a howitzer only to find myself in the middle of a voice controlled firing mission.

And then I heard the command "Fire!"

I was knocked off the tank's track wheels to a muddy patch of weeds several yards away where I lay motionless for the longest time and couldn't hear a thing.

Consider dangerous circumstances in life but also God's presence.

If only I had looked to the Lord for guidance beforehand, I wouldn't have entered an active firing zone. There was plenty of time to fix the phone.

If you don't know God, consider visiting a church, pastor, or reading God's word.

It may be that in a time of trouble, God will hear your plea for mercy and avoid a dangerous situation like I found myself in on the side of that tank.

The proverbs of Solomon, the son of David, king of Israel: To know wisdom and instruction; to perceive the words of understanding.   *Proverbs 1: 1*

Godly Sayings

The proverbs of Solomon contain wisdom and help guide us through life.

A wise man will hear, and will increase learning; and a man of understanding shall attain unto wise counsels (Prov. 1: 5).

Proverbs Chapters 1-9 are a preface to receiving instructions for life in Chapters 10-31.

The queen of Sheba had heard of Solomon's wisdom but wanted to see it for herself; so she travelled miles with gifts to visit and listened to his wisdom (1 Chron. 9).

There are also sayings in society that have proven to be worthy over time: haste makes waste, a bird in hand is worth two in the bush, never judge a book by its cover, or don't cry over spilt milk, among many others.

Each saying would be spoken at the right time.

While worldly sayings give us worldly wisdom, Biblical proverbs show us how to avoid evil, deal with strangers, have friends, and even gather riches.

Consider reading Proverbs for wisdom.

And out of the ground made the Lord God to grow every tree that is pleasant to the sight, and good for food; the tree of life also in the midst of the garden, and the tree of knowledge of good and evil.   *Genesis 2: 9*

Good and Evil

Here are the first words *good* and *evil* in the Bible.

A serpent devil represented *evil* and he tricked Eve into eating from a tree that God said not to eat from.

Eve thought it was *good*, so she gave it to her husband Adam and he ate.

After this disobedience to God, God showed up to discipline them because he loved them and didn't want them to get in any further trouble, for God is merciful.

Listen. God loves obedience. We don't have to understand what he wants -- just do it. The alternative is to receive God's discipline, and in this case, Eve was to bear children in sorrow and Adam was to work by the sweat of his face.

God's commandments are such that it will *go well with us* -- as the scripture says in Deuteronomy 6.

This obedience tree is where God is – like a heavenly throne of peace that extends far beyond time and space (see Rev. 22: 2).

And God's Son Jesus guards the tree of life.

He'll let us in the heavenly throne after we've confessed sins and come into agreement with God's will.

For thus saith the high and holy One who inhabiteth eternity, whose name is Holy: I dwell in the high and holy place, with him also who is of a contrite and humble spirit . . .

Isaiah 57: 15

Low to High

The above verse along within Isaiah chapters 56-58, show how to get close to God.

Before a person can stand up and be recognized as a person of faith, trust, and understanding, he must first bow down and listen to God in the spirit.

Then he can recognize the higher power of God.

This is where we need to be – low and humble -- to know the heights of God and to say, "This is who I am. I have a place here. And I have a special gift to the world that no one can duplicate because God is my director."

Jesus gives us a good example of being lowly, "Take my yoke upon you, and learn of me; for I am meek and lowly in heart, and ye shall find rest for unto your souls" (Matt. 11: 29).

After this yoke of Jesus is accepted, God becomes a guide for life.

Our words, actions, and the glory of God are governed by a God that will lead to peace, prosperity, and good health.

And not for that nation only, but that also he should gather together in one the children of God that were scattered abroad.   *John 11: 52*

Salvation for All

Believers in Jesus are scattered all over the face of the earth and unified in the faith and life of the resurrected Christ.

And Satan can't stand it.

Multiple attempts have been made to shut down churches, persecute Christians, and kill innocent believers -- all in the person of Satan stopping a movement that would incorporate righteousness in the public arena and love for humanity.

But how satisfying it is to join together and spread the good news of Jesus to people who know not, see not, or have heard not.

God would have his children be in foreign places to glorify and serve him.

Caiaphas, the high priest knew this; so he directed the path of Jesus to crucifixion, to not only provide a Savior for the Jewish nation but for other people as well.

Consider this action of sacrifice but also the gathering of believers all over the world to help and encourage people despite persecution, defamation, and unbelief.

The rule of God by Caiaphas shows just how much power God has over worldly authorities – to provide mercy through the blood of Jesus and redemption for sin.

Therefore, thus will I do unto thee, O Israel, and because I will do this unto thee, prepare to meet thy God, O Israel.

Amos 4: 12

A Sign of the Time

Judgment was coming to the people.

The prophet Amos was burdened over the sin of the northern kingdom of Israel in the eighth century B.C.; so he pronounced a decree: Prepare to meet thy God.

Prepare to meet thy God might be as good as any wording to get people's attention.

Such wording was on a church sign along Highway 57 in the Little River area of South Carolina. I assumed the sign lettering was put there by the preacher trying to get people to think about God.

Well, it did.

Cars would swerve and traffic would slow by the sign.

Who knows what effect the wording had on someone?

John the Baptist introduced a similar message in Matthew 3: 2 when the people needed a Savior for their sins: "Repent; for the Kingdom of Heaven is present."

And God provided Jesus as a sacrifice for sins.

Now in Shushan, the palace, there was a certain Jew, whose name was Mordecai, the son of Jair, the son of Shimei, the son of Kish, a Benjamite.   *Esther 2: 5*

Two Religions – One Victor

God is not mentioned in the Book of Esther.

But he is there: his law and presence delivered the Jewish people from a massacre.

Mordecai, a Jew, would not bow down to a foreign officer named Haman of the Persian army after a decree was made to kill all the Jews by the laws of the Persians and Medes.

Instead, Mordecai arose and went out into the center of the street and wailed.

Consider the cost of serving God: we are often threatened with violence, homelessness, and even death.

But by Esther's plea to the king and Mordecai's faith, the adversary Haman was hung from the gallows.

For unto the angels hath he not put in subjection the world to come, of which we speak.   *Hebrews 2: 5*

The Angel Divide

Not only do angels supervise matters in the world but they give strength to people, like what Jesus received when he was in agony at the Mount of Olives shortly before his death and an angel visited him (Luke 22: 43).

We also know a prophet was worn out after running away from Jezebel and ended up in a desert, where an angel visited him and gave him strength (1 Kings 19).

Consider the humble man Abraham, who was visited by three angels and hurriedly went to prepare food for them (Genesis 18: 1).

I received angelic help when I was young and sick with nowhere to go: an angel took me in for weeks and nursed me back to health.

But there are also fallen angels – ones who left their place of habitation and who are out performing the will of Satan (Rev. 20: 2).

Consider all these angels but also Jesus, who was made a little lower than the angels.

Jesus gives us salvation from sin and victory over Satanic angels.

"I am the way, the truth, and the life; no man cometh unto the Father, but by me.   John 14: 6

The Connection

There was a sale of used goods in a barn one day and on one aisle there was an old switchboard – which brought back memories of me operating one in the Army in the spring of 1972.

This switchboard was complete with jacks and wires – and cobwebs. It had been sitting idle somewhere for quite a long time.

But anyway, when our commander was using the field phone to direct firing missions with forward observers, I would connect the jacks in their respective holes to make the connection.

I tried it again on this old switchboard, for memory sakes, but of course there was no one on the other line.

Not anyone could just talk to the commander: they needed a code word.

It is the same with God: we got to by Jesus, who can take away our sins, to find God.

The code word for us is Jesus. Get by Jesus and then we can talk to the commander.

And they took up twelve baskets full of the fragments and of the fish.   *Mark 6: 43*

The Blessedness of Giving

The disciples gave out five loaves of barley and two fishes to a hungry crowd that had come from miles away to hear Jesus – and they received twelve baskets back.

That's what giving does – a blessing comes back.

Jesus proclaimed it in Luke 6: 38, "Give and it shall be given to you . . . ."

Consider one of my friends who went fishing and caught very few but came back with a container full.

It's because of his kindness. People see his love for God -- and they want to give back.

Commit yourself to serving God without any expectations (read Psalm 62:5).

It doesn't have to be understood; it's an action of faith, and one that pleases God.

When Jesus, therefore, saw his mother, and the disciple standing by, whom he loved, he saith unto his mother, "Woman, behold thy son!"   John 19: 26

Calling the Name

It was no accident Jesus called out the names of his mother and a disciple before death.

Mentioning these names *let go of them*, as he was about to give up the spirit and go to heaven.

This is what happens on the last day on earth: we let go of people and things to reach out for the heavenly throne of God where Jesus sits on the right side.

It's a mystery, but it could happen any time God wants it to happen.

Consider the disciples of Jesus; they had left jobs, families, and homes to follow him. And look at all the friendships they made as a result of them letting go! The people were subject unto them.

If you want a deeper personal relationship with God, consider letting go of people, places, and things.

Know God alone can meet your needs and give contentment (Philippians 4: 19).

Behold, thou desirest truth in the inward parts, and in the hidden part thou shalt make me know wisdom. Psalms 51:6

God's Hidden Works

I drove up to a bank teller's window and saw a five dollar bill in the tray. I looked up to see the teller staring at me.

"What's that for?" I asked.

She said, "You got any more of those books?"

I had given her a devotional book a month earlier.

"Sure," I said, and I grabbed a couple off the seat and put them in the tray.

"I want to hear something positive," she said. "The preacher at my church preaches a fire and brimstone message and how we're all going to hell if we don't repent."

"Probably true," I said. "But it's not his job to convict people of sin. That's the Holy Spirit's mission."

"Well, certainly," she said.

Jesus knew this, and when an adulteress and her accusers wanted to stone her, he quietly bowed his head and let God do the work (John 8).

According as we hearkened unto Moses in all things, so will we hearken unto thee; only the Lord thy God be with thee, as he was with Moses.   Joshua 1: 17

The God Check

The people did not know if their newly appointed leader Joshua would be a person who looked to God for the right way to travel, eat, and be safe from danger: Joshua had to prove God was with him.

So when Joshua lead them across the river Jordan into a land of promise, they knew God was with him.

And on that day the Lord magnified Joshua in the sight of all Israel.

The Bible says, Blessed is the nation whose God is the Lord; and the people he has chosen for his own inheritance (Psalms 33: 12).

How true that is, for God's ways are perfect.

But when a nation and its leaders turn away from God's presence, there will be harsh consequences.

That nation will become enslaved to another nation and false idols (Deut. 28: 36).

Blessed is the man that endureth temptation; for when he is tried, he shall receive the crown of life, which the Lord hath promised to them that love him.   James 1: 12

The Transformational Book of James

Temptation to sin is a daily occurrence that Christ has defeated by his power over Satan and the Book of James tells us how to apply this power in five chapters.

There are five precepts to follow: a person must eliminate negative or vain words of speech, be perfect in the law of liberty; resist temptations of evil; be doers of the word and not hearers only; and live by faith by the sacrificial blood of Jesus in the spirit of God.

Millions of books on shelves all over the world can not provide such guidance to life in five short chapters.

The Christian life, though marked for persecution by the anti-Christ, is acceptable to God for eternal worship and security at the throne of heaven and should be sought in a world of hopelessness, discouragement, and vanity.

With Jesus there is life, and James shows us how to get there.

For as often as ye eat this bread, and drink this cup, you do show the Lord's death till he come.   1 Cor. 11:26

The Lord's Supper

The Apostle Paul encourages us to be in remembrance of Christ's death on the cross as a sacrifice for our sins by participating in what is commonly referred to as the Lord's Supper, or Communion, in the church.

A woman came into a used goods store the other day not looking for anything special until she saw a small drinking glass which was about 3" tall with a round bottom base and fluted stem.

She looked at me. "This is a communion glass," and she held it up proudly. "Communion is a mystery."

But it's not really a mystery.

The Apostle Paul said for a person to first examine himself to be worthy of taking communion. In other words, make sure any sin is addressed or confessed before communing with the Lord.

This action breaks the condemnation of worldly ways (v. 32).

And then there is peace with God.

And it shall be when the Lord thy God shall have brought thee into the land . . . to give thee great and goodly cities, which though buildest not, and houses . . . Deut. 6: 10-11

Change of Mind

Moses at one time told the people they would inherit houses to live in they had not built – that God was going to provide these homes at no cost.

I always wondered who owned these giveaway homes and how the occupants would feel about foreigners taking over their property.

Either someone complained or Moses came to his senses. Or maybe God came along and corrected him because Moses later said his people were to build their own houses (Deut. 8: 12).

Jesus changed his mind once – about the scribes in Matthew 23 – blaming them as hypocrites -- but later he grouped them with prophets and wise men that Pharisees had killed and how their blood stained the conscience (v. 34).

Consider our statements that can lead to misunderstandings but also know that correction comes through God for truth and righteousness.

Proverbs 17: 27 may be a guide for us: He that hath knowledge spareth his words; and a man of understanding is of an excellent spirit.

Blessed are they who do hunger and thirst after righteousness, for they shall be filled.   Matthew 5: 6

Filled

Searching for righteousness is pleasing to God.

Consider Solomon's prayer in 1Kings 3:9-14. Solomon asked the Lord for discernment of good and bad, and God *fulfilled* the request.

Jesus fulfilled a prophet's vision of God sending a Savior to earth in form of man to be a sacrifice for sin, a conqueror over evil, and a resurrected being into heaven that would prepare a place for his believers to be free from the fear of death.

Consider believing in Christ who rose from the dead. Upon confession of sin and receiving forgiveness by God, we become filled – by the Holy Ghost.

The Apostles were filled by the Holy Spirit (Acts 2: 4) on Pentecost, the fiftieth day after Passover when the Holy Spirit descended from heaven and filled the apostles with gifts of the spirit.

But we don't have to wait fifty days.

Christ is available now for salvation and life.

Oh, how love I thy law! It is my mediation all the day.
Psalms 119: 97

A Time for Courage

After taking care of some business one day at the beach, I stopped by the library in Little River to get a couple of books.

I walked into the multi-office building through the door at the magistrate's side of the building. As I walked near that office, I saw a friend slumped over in a chair crying.

"What's wrong?" I asked.

"He's going to kill me," she said.

I was slightly familiar with her situation hearing about someone stalking her.

"So you're filing a complaint?" I said.

"Yes. I have to face this sometime. The office opens in a couple minutes."

I agreed that she should do so, and after another cry, we both prayed about the matter and entered the magistrate's office.

At some time in life, trials such as what this young lady was experiencing happen, though maybe in a different place.

A stand has to be taken for what is right.

To ignore such problems and think they will just go away is not the best way to live: the victim will be in bondage to fear.

Knowing God and Jesus allows us to face problems and overcome them by righteous precepts.

And we know that people who forsake the law -- praise the wicked (Proverbs 28;4).

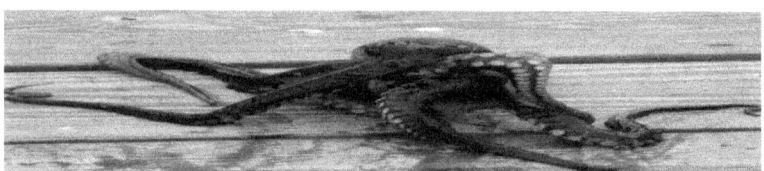

> .*And Moses went up unto God, and the Lord called unto him out of the mountain, saying, Thus shalt thou say to the house of Jacob, and tell the children of Israel . . .*
>
> Ex. 19: 3

The Order

God gave a direct order to Moses to make some laws that would help guide the people to a good place.

A direct order is sometimes used by a high ranking soldier in the military who wants something done.

But God incorporated mercy in his order: he not only gave the people a warning about approaching Mount Sinai, but mentioned they "might" do his commandments that it would go well with them (see Deut. 6).

Consider harsh orders that restrict our willingness to perform work.

Jesus condemned such orders from scribes and Pharisees (Matthew 23) – said they were issuing orders but weren't taking part in them. Prophets, wise men, and scribes were being killed.

Go to court today and more than likely a lawyer will want an order signed.

Fortunately, Moses got his order straight from a divine judge, and that's who we should seek for direction and life.

A proverb says, Pleasant words are like a honeycomb; sweet to the soul, and health to the bones (Prov. 16: 24).

That makes us want to perform the order.

Forever, O Lord, thy word is settled in heaven. Thy faithfulness is unto all generations; thou hast established the earth, and it abideth.

Psalms 119: 89-90

The Enduring Word

At the auction barn one day, there was an old Bible sitting on a table.

The cover was in immaculate condition and the pages looked as if they had never been turned – and the binding was secure. Upon opening the first few pages, I discovered the Bible was 52 years old, having been published in 1970.

It was a Bible printed by Fireside Publishing Company of Wichita, Kansas, for the Catholic Church.

But consider the people who surrounded this Bible as it lay dormant. Possibly they were illiterate, or maybe they were working in the fields and there was no time for reading, or maybe they rejected the word of God altogether!

But I was certainly thankful to find this Bible.

There was a center reference section with scriptures on each page that showed when each individual book was written, Hebrew and Greek translated references, and twelve pictures of Christ's disciples.

God's printed word of life was here, and though it was fifty years old, it had the same words as in today's Bible.

Thy word is a lamp unto my feet, a light unto my path. Psalms 119: 105).

The Right Path

It's easy to wander off a path and look at pretty flowers, animals, or talk to other people. Or maybe adverse weather has muddied the path and it is necessary to walk around wet areas.

As many did, I used to walk along the Oconaluftee River in Cherokee, N.C. daily where I would stop and look at a patch of blooming stonecrop, crow's foot (salad greens), or fiddler ferns that were budding upward -- not to mention listening to the thundering waters of the river nearby after a rainstorm.

But God's commandments keep us on the right path.

Following God's ways with gladness of heart allows us to see his manifest of works in nature.

There's an old saying about resting from work occasionally and smelling the roses, but we should also take time to know that God is always present and will lead us properly.

Humble yourselves, therefore, under the mighty hand of God, that he may exalt you in due time, casting all your care upon him; for he careth for you.   *1 Peter 5: 7*

God Cares

Pastor Bill Monroe of Florence Baptist Temple in Florence, South Carolina preaches on a delayed television broadcast every Saturday night.

One sermon was on Psalms 142, where David is hiding in a cave from King Saul who is out to kill him.

David's prayer said, "No one cares for my soul."

How relevant is that when the world seems like it is crashing down and there is no one to help.

Certainly God cares for the soul, or he would not have created us.

This is our confidence.

When separated from friends or family, being persecuted, or sense danger, God is ever present for comfort and direction.

God said for us to worship him in the place he chooses, and sometimes that is within the cave of thoughts and worry.

And Jesus said, "I am with you always, even unto the end of the age," (Matthew 28: 20).

Trust in the Lord with all thine heart, and lean not unto thine own understanding. *Proverbs 3: 5*

The Right Time

There are times when certain projects should not be attempted like mowing grass in the rain, travelling on ice, or painting outdoors on a rainy day.

Attempting such projects would only make things worse.

It is the same with God.

Attempt something without his leading and there is sure failure or vanity.

The Bible says, Except the Lord builds the house, they labor in vain that build it . . . (Psalms 127: 1).

Forbearing to grieve God is one secret to producing good work, along with getting to know him through Jesus our Savior.

If things do go wrong, Jesus has died for our errors to bring us into agreement with God's will. The right time to find God is when a cup of sin overflows and there is a need for salvation.

Jesus addressed this situation and said to bring fruits worthy of repentance.

And I will remember my covenant, which is between me and you and every living creature of all flesh; and the waters shall no more become a flood to destroy all flesh.
Genesis 9: 15

God's Promise to Man and Animals

God made a covenant with the righteous man Noah that there would be no more floods that destroyed life (Genesis 9).

Fortunately, Noah saved some animals and they multiplied, but now there are thousands of animals and birds on an endangered species list.

While a wolf and lamb may live together as a symbol of peace between people of different beliefs in Isaiah 11: 26 through the birth of Jesus Christ, large numbers of animals are dying from being hit by vehicles, shot by guns, or die as by-products of hunters – especially the fish and mollusks of the sea which get caught up in nets.

Man may find himself on an endangered species list if the use of artificial radiation from satellites, tower antennas, and appliances are not limited.

But consider the wildlife that God had created, it took two days for God to create them. And God said animals will be in fear of man (Gen. 9: 2).

The preacher in Ecclesiastes addressed the beasts of the field and said that man does not have pre-eminence over them – for all go to the same place upon death (Eccl. 3:19).

A righteous man regardeth the life of his beast . . . (Proverbs 12: 10).

For whom the Lord loveth he correcteth, as a father the son in whom he delighteth. *Proverbs 3: 12*

The Blessing of Correction

Imagine what it would be like if we didn't get corrected for doing something wrong: we would be working in vain.

But hearing or reading God's word gets us right -- as long we aren't stubborn to being reproved (Proverbs 1: 20-33)

God doesn't have to take the time to correct us when we've done something wrong, but he does it because he loves us.

We must only turn to him to learn the right way and be remorseful enough to admit we've made a mistake.

But everyone makes mistakes.

Know that God has provided his son Jesus to give us mercy in time of need, especially in correction.

All scripture is given by inspiration of God, and is profitable for doctrine, for reproof, for correction, for instruction in righteousness.   2 Timothy 3: 16

Bible Revisions

Most Bible translators and editors rely on the above scripture to make new Bibles, versions of the Bible, and commentaries of the Bible.

Sometimes inaccuracies in a Bible -- from whichever original version that has been chosen to be translated –are fixed due to new archaeological discoveries.

Few people admit the Bible has inconsistencies -- like the Broadman's Commentary expositors who were forced to understand such statements as "the evening and the morning were the first day" in Genesis 1 – when the sun and the 24 hour day had not yet been created until the fourth day.

Of course, that brings a litany of questions about the sun already being here and clouds blocking the light.

There are many such instances of Bible inconsistencies.

But the Bible is not a scientific book: It is a book about man's humanness and a divine God who loves man.

Humanness is indicated in God's first command to Adam and Eve about not eating from the tree of knowledge of good and evil – the verb "know" has sexual connotations.

As far as darkness and light are concerned, there is no darkness or light in the river of life that proceeds from God's throne in the Book of Revelation 22: 1-5.

Consider contradictions in the scriptures but the nature of God to test man's resolve to find truth and understanding about life.

And the Word was made flesh, and dwelt among us (and we beheld his glory, the glory as of the only begotten of the Father), full of grace and truth.   John 1: 14

Jesus the Human

Jesus is often thought of as a spiritual being that rose from the dead after being crucified and now sits on the right hand side of God.

But consider the human things that Jesus did on earth: he read the scriptures; he rode a donkey, he distributed bread and wine to eat and drink; he got a foot massage; he physically tired from a long journey; and he became emotionally drained before going to court.

He experienced a lot of what we do.

Fortunately, Jesus' words in scriptures have been passed down through the ages to give us guidance.

While Jesus the Savior is a redeemer of sin, his human actions on earth were inspirational and truly blessed by God to give an example of healing, teaching, and ministering to people for God to be glorified.

And I say also unto thee, "That thou are Peter, and upon this rock I will build my church, and the gates of Hades shall not prevail against it."   *Matt. 16: 18*

The Church

With this one statement, Jesus Christ established the church. And it's no coincidence Jesus was talking to a sinner, Simon, son of Jonah.

The church is a gathering place for believers but also for sinners like Simon, who doubted Jesus would die for the people's sins.

The church is a healing institution, where man finds freedom and guidance to find the living God through Jesus.

I visited a church near Tabor City, N.C. one weekend.

I settled in to listen to a man preach about Mark 3, where a man got healed by Jesus despite criticism from the congregation in front of Jesus.

Discouragement took place thousands of years ago in the church and it continues today.

But consider the church, though its leaders and Jesus get criticized, is open to anyone looking for help and repentance from sin.

The pastor at this church said, "I've been in church all my life! Even before I was born, I was in church, because my mother carried me there when I was in the womb!"

I thought, *Well, that sounds like Jesus!*

And the pastor preached a wonderful sermon.

Freedom from sin's bondage may be just a church away but also know Jesus, who despite criticism is always present.

.

As for God, his way is perfect; the word of the Lord is proved; he is a shield to all those who trust in him.
Psalms 18: 30

Turtle Time

In the spring and fall of the year turtles exit hibernation areas to soak up sunshine.

Many times they will lay on asphalt roads, such as the three turtles I saw one day in different places.

They not only get heat from above but from below, because asphalt absorbs heat.

Two were box turtles, and the other looked like a yellow slider.

But consider the turtle, which sits still and soaks up the sun like we should be absorbing God's word.

The Bible says, My son, keep my words, and lay up my commandments with thee. Keep my commandments, and live, and my law as the apple of thine eye. Bind them upon thy fingers, write them upon the table of thine heart (Proverbs 7: 1-3).

A good place to start binding the word on the soul is in the Book of John because it contains simple words and introduces the Son of God, Jesus, who takes away sins.

But we should not forget to read the law of God in the Book of Exodus, Deuteronomy, Leviticus, and Numbers; for the law of the Lord is perfect, converting the soul; Psalms 19: 7.

For whatever things were written in earlier times were written, for our learning, that we, through patience and comfort of the scriptures, might have hope. Romans 15: 5

Life's Answers

Years ago, I was going through some depression when God instructed me to write a book about the subject.

He also told me to seek out my deliverance, and that's exactly what I did.

"Ask, and it shall be given you; seek, and ye shall find; knock, and it shall be opened unto you," Jesus said in Matthew 7: 7.

When you are struggling in an area of life, consider researching the scriptures to find the answer to the problem. Read books and listen to sermons about it. And pray.

God is faithful to give you the answers if you look for them and seek.

Consider also getting a concordance to Bible words, a Bible dictionary or expository, and a commentary to see what other people say about the subject.

Know the simplicity of our faith, as the prophet Micah has stated in Micah 6: 8: He hath shown thee, O man, what is good; and what doth the Lord require of thee, but to do justly, and to love mercy, and to walk humbly with thy God.

Jeanette Cole

The Need for God, Part II

People are dying from disease in record numbers.

Animals are scattered dead along roadways after days of chemical spraying by the military, county, and private industry. One day, I counted 15 dead along 20 miles of road. Possum, raccoons, birds, cats, dogs, foxes, a bear, skunks, squirrels, are some of the animals I have seen lying dead along roads after a weekend of heavy air spraying and vehicular traffic coming to and from the beach areas.

The weather is more volatile than ever with harsh storms -- and flooding -- where it normally doesn't.

There's a lot of heat in the atmosphere with strong radiation fields emanating from cell phone tower antennas, microwave repeaters, and lighting equipment. Ionizing radiation gases flood the atmosphere from nuclear plants.

Animals and humans are not only becoming confused by the influx of radiation but their immune systems are breaking down. It is too much stress, and leaves life open to infection and disease.

Combine this with neurotoxins in foods and a demonized technology that can affect the moods and thoughts of people all over the world invites disaster, bad health, and death.

For these reasons, we need God.

God's laws in the scriptures can help us. We are to be holy as God is holy. Many problems will disappear if we seek God's holiness. In addition, we all need the mercy of Jesus Christ, who died for our sins.

Consider that God's ways have proven to be right in the past, as people testified that God freed them from slavery, chaos, and death.

It's time to call on God to become free of satanic oppression, pollution, and false idols.

Kenneth M. Lee, 2023

www.ingramcontent.com/pod-product-compliance
Lightning Source LLC
LaVergne TN
LVHW021713080426
835510LV00010B/980